# WORKING CAPITAL MANAGEMENT

# Financial Management Association

## SURVEY AND SYNTHESIS SERIES

# WORKING CAPITAL MANAGEMENT

Lorenzo A. Preve
Virginia Sarria-Allende

OXFORD
UNIVERSITY PRESS
2010

# OXFORD
## UNIVERSITY PRESS

Oxford University Press, Inc., publishes works that further
Oxford University's objective of excellence
in research, scholarship, and education.

Oxford   New York
Auckland   Cape Town   Dar es Salaam   Hong Kong   Karachi
Kuala Lumpur   Madrid   Melbourne   Mexico City   Nairobi
New Delhi   Shanghai   Taipei   Toronto

With offices in
Argentina   Austria   Brazil   Chile   Czech Republic   France   Greece
Guatemala   Hungary   Italy   Japan   Poland   Portugal   Singapore
South Korea   Switzerland   Thailand   Turkey   Ukraine   Vietnam

Copyright © 2010 by Oxford University Press, Inc.

Published by Oxford University Press, Inc.
198 Madison Avenue, New York, New York 10016
www.oup.com

Oxford is a registered trademark of Oxford University Press

Library of Congress Cataloging-in-Publication Data

Preve, Lorenzo A.
Working capital management / Lorenzo Preve
and Virginia Sarria-Allende.
p.   cm. — (Financial management association survey and synthesis series)
Includes bibliographical references and index.
ISBN 978-0-19-973741-3
1. Working capital.   I. Sarria-Allende, Virginia.   II. Title.
HG4028.W65P74 2010
658.15'244dc22     2009030286

9 8 7 6 5 4 3 2 1

Printed in the United States of America
on acid-free paper

# Preface

The importance of working capital management became clear to us several years ago. There were two main reasons for this fact. First, we live, do research, teach, and work with firms in an emerging market, in which a sound working capital management can explain the difference between a financially distressed and a profitable firm. Second, we have been fortunate to have a great team of colleagues in the finance department at IAE Business School who have been thinking about and discussing these issues with us for a while. Javier García Sanchez, José Luis Gomez Lopez Egea, Guillermo Fraile, Gabriel Noussan, Florencia Paolini and Martín Pérez de Solay have contributed a great deal in shaping the ideas that eventually made their way to the pages of this book.

Several professors throughout our formal finance education shaped the way we think about corporate finance, and part of their contribution can probably be traced in the pages that follow.

A considerable number of MBA students and executives have been exposed, along the past several years, to the discussion in this book. The interaction with them, their interest and passion, and their real-life examples and cases surely helped us to refine and redefine the ideas that we present in this book. We are indebted to them all.

Finally, we would like to thank our families for supporting us unconditionally.

# Contents

# Introduction

In this book, we discuss the decision of operating investment and the corresponding financing, one of the most strategic issues in modern corporate finance. This discussion, mostly ignored by academics until recent years, becomes extremely important when firms expand beyond the boundaries of efficient financial markets. Most models in corporate finance understand a firm as a set of assets financed by either financial debt or equity. Even though this standard framework is useful for analyzing many financial decisions, it might be misleading to guide the crucial decision of how to define and finance the operating investments of a firm.

We focus on these aspects of corporate finance by addressing several important factors. In Chapter 1, we start by presenting the fundamental framework of corporate finance and the basic financial statements generated by a firm. This chapter helps to set the stage, introducing some key concepts that will be widely used throughout the rest of the book. In the second and third chapters, we specifically address the essential understanding of working capital management. We start, in Chapter 2, by explaining the traditional definition of working capital and continue by challenging the standard interpretation and use of the concept. Next, we provide a more comprehensive framework to think about working capital management. More specifically, we identify the two basic components:

the investment and the financing components. The investment component, called financial needs for operation (FNOs), represents the operating investment of the firm. The financing component corresponds to the concept of working capital. In Chapter 3, we study how the size of the operating investment changes according to the activity level of the firm. Subsequently, we analyze how the firm should finance this investment depending on whether it results from growth or permanent change in trade conditions, or from seasonal variations. It is important to notice that we constantly shift between investment and financing considerations; one of the main contributions of this book is precisely the emphasis on the relevance of this link when analyzing business strategy. In Chapter 4, we combine the concepts discussed in the first three chapters to perform a complete financial analysis. We reorganize all the available information following the traditional ratio analysis and then suggest its use in an integrated analytical framework.

The next four chapters are dedicated to the study of the main components of the operating investment of the firm: cash, receivables, inventories, and payables. In Chapter 5, we discuss the reasons why firms hold cash, analyzing some of the traditional cash models in corporate finance. Chapter 6 addresses the main implications of investing in clients' financing. It discusses the financing provided to clients, the reasons why firms decide to provide such financing, and the importance of credit risk management. In Chapter 7, we discuss the importance of inventory management. Inventories are an important operating decision of the firm, with deep implications in profitability and financing. Finally, we review the main theories of inventory management. Last, in Chapter 8, we move to the other side of the balance sheet and analyze the financing provided by suppliers. Even if trade credit can be an expensive financing tool, firms still decide to use it extensively. Together, chapters 6 and 8 provide a review and general discussion of the main theories of trade credit.

Chapter 9 discusses the role of short-term debt in financing the operating investment. Short-term debt is considered to play a buffer role in financing the temporary operating investments of the firm. Additionally, the chapter provides a discussion of the main sources of short-term financial debt.

In chapters 10–12, we emphasize the strategic perspective of working capital. In Chapter 10, we discuss the role of working capital management as a strategic tool. We provide an integrated view of working capital policies, and we discuss how they can be used to help improve firms' competitive position. Chapter 11 deals with strategic issues from the financing perspective. It discusses the cost of capital of the long-term financing of operating assets. Long-term financing, composed of long-term debt and equity, has a cost that needs to be considered by top management in order to make sound financial decisions. Finally, Chapter 12 discusses some of the observed patterns in working capital around the world.

This is an important book for general managers who need to understand the corporate financial framework. Many books and articles discuss the big corporate financing decisions; the financial impact of day-to-day business decisions, however, has been frequently ignored. This book aims at closing that gap. Therefore, this is a book for functional managers who need to understand the financial consequences of their operating decisions; this book will show managers (not only financial managers) how each managerial decision shapes the finance position, the cash flow, and, consequently, the profitability of the firm. This text is written, to a large extent, in a casual and nonformal language so as to make it available to a wide array of readers. No basic prior knowledge of financial, mathematical, or statistical concepts is needed to understand the message we intend to convey.

# WORKING CAPITAL MANAGEMENT

# 1

# Corporate Finance

## THE BASIC CORPORATE FINANCE FRAMEWORK

Most businesses are started by an investor who is willing to invest his or her capital in exchange for a return on the investment. How much of a return? As financial economists would say, the riskier the investment is, the higher the expected return.

The money that the investor uses to start the firm is referred to as the firm's initial capital. This money is invested in what is called the firm's assets, which include everything from the most obvious items such as property, plant, and equipment, inventory, and cash, to less obvious items such as customers' financing. In some cases, especially in the case of small firms, the investor makes all of the firm's investment decisions. In other cases, particularly as firms grow, other people—the firm's management—are tasked with making these decisions.

Aiming to meet investors' expected returns, after selecting an optimal investment the business must use the investment to produce goods and/or services that will be sold to customers. In generating these sales, a firm will incur several costs, for example, materials and production costs, storage and distribution costs, employee-related costs, and taxes. What is left after collecting revenues and paying the related costs is the firm's *profit,* which is the basis for estimating the investors' return on investment.

Thus far we have focused attention on "an investor" who decides to apply his or her money to a given business. In reality, however, most businesses do not count on a single investor to finance the entirety of their assets; rather, they typically have many investors. These investors are not all alike. For our purposes here, investors can be characterized according to the type of contract they establish with the firm.

Broadly speaking, we can categorize these contracts into two basic types: *debt contracts* and *equity contracts*.[1] A debt contract is one in which the firm schedules a promised repayment to the investor. The owners of the corresponding claim are called *debt holder*s. An equity contract, in contrast, is a contract in which the firm assigns to investors what can be considered the firm's *residual profit,* that is, the profit that is left over after the firm covers its operating costs and its obligations to debt holders. The owners of the latter type of claim are named *equity holders*. Figure 1.1 illustrates this framework.

To summarize, a firm's main business activities consist of identifying optimal investments, arranging appropriate financing to sustain the investment, and using the selected investments to generate revenues from which operating expenses, debt obligations, and equity holders' returns are paid. These activities are summarized in a firm's financial statements, which are the set of documents that collect and organize this information. We discuss the two most basic financial statements next.

## FINANCIAL STATEMENTS

A firm's main business activities as described previously are recorded in two basic financial statements: (1) the balance sheet and (2) the income

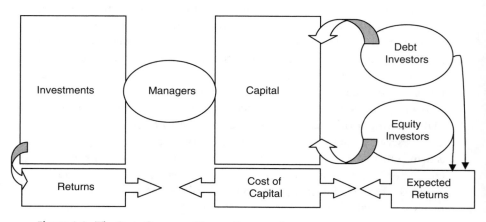

**Figure 1.1.** The Basic Corporate Finance Framework

statement. In the following paragraphs, we describe both the primary characteristics of each financial report taken separately and the interaction between the two statements. This interaction is important as it allows analysts to get a more complete picture of a company's financial situation and business performance.

## The Balance Sheet

The balance sheet provides a snapshot of the firm at a given moment in time. This report has two main parts: the left-hand side, which presents the *assets* of the firm, and the right-hand side, which shows the corresponding *liabilities*. The assets represent the investments made by the firm, whereas the liabilities characterize the way those assets have been financed. It is easy to see that both parts of the balance sheet reflect two sides of the same coin: one cannot be affected without altering the other, and both have the same size (i.e., the assets are equal to the liabilities). For example, if we make a new investment, it is either because we have obtained new financing that allows for it (increasing both assets, reflecting the investment, and liabilities, reflecting the financing), or because we have funded it with the proceeds of a divestiture of a previous investment (leaving the total amount of assets and liabilities unchanged). Similarly, if we obtain new financing, we can accumulate cash or buy goods or equipment (increasing both assets and liabilities), or we can use the money to cancel some previous claim (leaving the total figures unchanged).

The items reported on a balance sheet are presented in an order that follows convention. In particular, assets are organized by liquidity (i.e., the ease with which a given asset can be converted into cash), and liabilities are organized based on exigibility (i.e., when each liability is due).[2] On the asset side, items are sorted by descending liquidity, with the most liquid assets at the top of the list and the least liquid ones at the bottom.[3] According to this rule, a firm's assets could plausibly be ordered as follows: cash, bank accounts, marketable securities, trade receivables, inventories, and, at the very bottom, property, plant, and equipment (PPE). Note that these assets are grouped into two broad categories: short-term or *current assets,* which are expected to become liquid within one year, and fixed or *noncurrent assets,* which are expected to take more than a year to become liquid. Short-term assets often include items such as cash, banking accounts, trade receivables, and inventories, and typical noncurrent assets include PPE and goodwill.

On the liabilities side of the balance sheet, the accounts are classified based on exigibility, with the most exigible claim (the claim due soonest) presented at the top and the least exigible claim (the furthest-dated claim) listed at the bottom. The least exigible claim consists of equity, since equity holders receive their part after all other obligations have been satisfied. Long-term debt is listed above equity, and before long-term debt are the different sources of short-term financing. Typically, the first type of obligation listed is commercial credit, which consists of obligations the firm has with suppliers who sell their goods or services to the firm on credit, as such obligations are usually due within a number of days. Wages and other obligations due to employees in exchange for labor and managerial services are often listed next, as such payments are usually made on a monthly basis, with employees effectively extending short-term credit to the firm. Also included among the short-term liabilities are taxes owed to the government, which are accrued based on profit generation but only exigible on a monthly or quarterly basis, and payments owed on financial debt such as short-term bank loans or commercial paper.

Figure 1.2 provides an example of a representative firm's balance sheet.

As we mentioned earlier, the balance sheet provides a *snapshot* of a firm's investments and corresponding financing at a given point in time. One can take such snapshots on a monthly, quarterly, yearly, or other periodic basis and then compare these snapshots to analyze the evolution of the firm's investments and financing over time. When analyzing a firm's investments, we care about not only the size of total investments but also their main drivers—the inferences we draw about what is happening to a firm that is showing an increase in its trade receivables might be dramatically different from those we reach about a firm that is

| **Current Assets** | **Current Liabilities** |
| Cash & Bank Accounts | Suppliers |
| Trade Receivables | Employees |
| Inventories | ST Financial Debt |
| Other Current Assets | Taxes |
| | **Noncurrent Liabilities** |
| **Noncurrent Assets** | LT Financial Debt |
| Goodwill | Other LT Liab. |
| PP&E | |
| Other LT Assets | **Shareholders' Equity** |

**Figure 1.2.** The Balance Sheet

observing an increase in inventories. Similarly, when analyzing the evolution of, say, a growing firm's financing, it is important to look at whether the growth has been financed with (short- or long-term) debt or equity, as the financing choice will significantly impact a company's performance and risk exposure.

The previous discussion suggests that analysis of a firm's balance sheets can reveal extremely rich and interesting insights on the firm's performance. However, in order to have a more complete understanding of the firm's evolution, we need to have information on what has happened between consecutive reports. For example, changes in inventory across balance sheets are linked to how much the firm has bought and sold between report dates, and changes in equity financing are related to the amount of net income the firm has been able to generate. Information on firm activity between balance sheets can be obtained by looking at the second basic financial statement, the income statement, which is also called the profit and loss statement, or the P&L statement for short. One can think of the income statement as the *movie* that tells the story of the company between each pair of balance sheet *snapshots*.

## The Income Statement

The income statement is a representation of a firm's normal business operations between two consecutive balance sheet statements. In particular, it records the firm's total sales and costs incurred over the period, from which the firm's net income (or profit) is calculated. As is the case for balance sheets, the income statement can be prepared for any desired period of time (a week, a month, a quarter, a year, etc.). Typically, a one-year interval is used for tax and most legal purposes, but many firms also use quarterly or monthly income statements for different types of supplementary analysis. Later in the chapter we discuss the various components of a firm's income statement and then turn to the derivation of net income (profit).

The first item reported on an income statement is the firm's total sales, which is computed by adding all the invoices generated over the period. It is important to notice that at this stage we do not take into account whether these invoices have been paid or are still outstanding; we will consider this distinction in a subsequent chapter.[4]

Next, the income statement records the costs of the goods sold over the period. This item includes, among other things, those expenditures directly related to producing the goods that have been sold over the period, for instance, the raw materials used to produce these goods. Note that expenditures incurred over the period that are related to goods that were not sold but that are stored as inventory (either as raw material or as intermediate or final goods) are not counted as costs in the income state-ment; instead, these expenditures are recorded as assets, since they are regarded as an investment that will allow the firm to generate future sales.

To illustrate this distinction, consider the case of a firm that produces dining room sets. Assume that in the period under analysis, say a month, the firm produces and sells 5 dining room sets, each using 40 pounds of wood. The firm's total sales for the month will equal the 5 dining room sets sold over the month times the price per dining room set sold, and the firm's cost of goods sold will equal 40 pounds of wood times the cost of the wood per pound times the 5 dining room sets that have been sold. No problem so far, as we are making the important assumption that the firm bought the exact amount of wood needed to produce the items sold over the period. What happens, however, if we relax this assumption? Imagine now that the firm purchased enough wood to produce 10 dining room sets, but continued to produce and sell only 5 dining room sets. In this case, the firm would show the same total sales and the same cost of goods sold as before, but would now also show an increase in wood stored in inventory. The expenditure associated with this surplus wood is recorded an asset, as this wood will allow the firm to produce more din-ing room sets to be sold in the future. Note that it does not matter whether this surplus wood was acquired intentionally as an investment in future production capabilities or unintentionally as a result of weaker sales than expected—the accounting implications for the cost of goods sold and inventory are identical.

Other costs recorded in the income statement include the costs of keeping the company operational. Some of these costs vary with the level of production, whereas others are independent of production levels and are said to be fixed. Regardless of whether variable or fixed, these operat-ing costs are recognized on the basis of their relation with the sales and other business activity generated during the period, not on the basis of whether they have been paid during the period. Other financial reports, as we will see when we turn to sources and uses of funds, concentrate on actual cash flows.

We are now ready to discuss the derivation of a firm's net income. The first two lines of the income statement present the firm's total sales and corresponding cost of goods sold (CGS), which includes raw materials, labor, and variable operating costs. Subtracting CGS from sales gives the firm's gross margin, which is the income obtained before deducting any fixed costs.[5] Subtracting fixed costs from the gross margin gives earnings before interest and taxes (EBIT), and subtracting interest expenses from EBIT yields earnings before taxes (EBT). After deducting taxes, we get the firm's bottom line, that is, its net income or profit.

| | Net Sales |
|---|---|
| Minus | Cost of Goods Sold |
| | **Gross Profit (or Contribution Margin)** |
| Minus | Fixed Costs |
| | **EBIT** |
| Minus | Interest Expenses |
| | **Income Before Taxes** |
| Minus | Income Taxes |
| | **Net Income** |

**Figure 1.3.** The Income Statement

The sample income statement shown in Figure 1.3 illustrates how a firm's net income, or profit, is calculated.

As these discussions suggest, there is a strong connection between balance sheets and income statements—a change to one automatically affects the other. Understanding this interaction is crucial to reach a sound conclusion about business performance and profitability.

To recap so far, we have shown that the firm invests in assets that are used to produce goods and services that will be sold to customers, and that this production process has embedded costs. The P&L statement shows the accounting profit generated by the firm's operation. Since investors are paid from such profit, clearly this measure is of interest to investors. However, profit is not the only measure of interest, as it is not always a good proxy for the wealth generated by a given investment. In particular, investors also care about the cash flows of the firm. More specifically, investors consider the amount of cash that they invested and compare this value with the amount of cash that the investment returns to them, or their return on investment. We discuss this measure next.

## RETURN ON INVESTMENT

When cash enters the company from sales, management distributes the cash among the firm's various claim holders.[6] The first group of claim holders to be paid consists of employees and suppliers. After this group of claim holders has been satisfied, the remaining cash is distributed among financial claim holders. First among such claim holders are debt holders, who are paid in accordance with the seniority of their claim and the terms of the firm's debt contracts. Next in line is the federal tax authority, which has a claim on the firm's profit. Finally, after paying employees, suppliers, debt holders, and the tax authority, the balance is distributed to equity holders, who are also called shareholders. Note that this does not mean

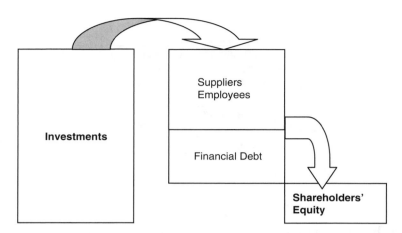

**Figure 1.4.** The Distribution of the Firm's Cash Flows

that the shareholders will receive all of the cash that remains after the firm's other obligations are met. Rather, the company will have set a dividend policy that depends, among other things, on the firm's industry and financial condition. This policy will allocate to equity holders a dividend distribution. The balance is held to be reinvested in the firm.[7]

Figure 1.4 illustrates the distribution of a firm's cash receipts, and in particular how an investor's return on investment is determined. Note that the arrows show the direction of the firm's cash flows according to the seniority of claims.

From the previous discussion, it is clear how financial investors are paid from the cash flows that the firm generates. The remaining question is whether the payment received is high enough to satisfy investors' ex ante expected returns. We briefly discuss this issue in the next section.

## INVESTORS' EXPECTED RETURN—THE COST OF CAPITAL

At the beginning of this chapter, we stated that investors are willing to invest their capital in exchange for a return, where the expected return increases with the risk of the investment. From the previous discussion on the allocation of generated cash flows, it is clear that different claim holders bear different levels of risk. For instance, while employees, suppliers, and debt holders enjoy a *promise* to be paid according to a schedule of payments, shareholders have no such promise; instead, given their subordinate claims, they are entitled to some return only after everyone else has been paid. As a result, shareholders clearly have higher risk exposure than other, higher priority claim holders.

Given that different claim holders have different degrees of risk, how can we characterize the return requirements of different investors? Consider an investor bearing no risk. This investor would be expected to require the risk-free rate of return. Now consider an investor who invests on a risky asset. Given that this investor can always obtain a risk-free return (simply by buying a U.S. Treasury bond), he or she would not be willing to accept a return lower than the risk-free rate. Moreover, the investor will require a premium over the risk-free rate to agree to invest in the risky asset, as otherwise could obtain the risk-free rate at lower risk by investing in the risk-free asset. Note that investment risk varies not only by type of claim on the firm but also across firms, industries, and countries. Thus, expected returns will vary along these dimensions, too.

Based on the previous arguments, we can express investors' expected return in general form as follows:

$$Expected\ Return = R_f + Risk\ Premium,$$

where $R_f$ is the return promised by a risk-free investment and risk premium is the extra return that an investor requires for an investment with a given level of risk. However, since debt holders and equity holders take different risks, their risk premium will certainly differ. Thus, when thinking about expected returns, the two most common approaches are to consider either the combined expected return of debt and equity holders as a group or the expected return of shareholders alone.

To consider the expected return of shareholders alone, let the cost of equity be denoted by $K_e$. We can then say that equity holders' expected return is given by:

$$K_e = R_f + Risk\ Premium_e.$$

For completeness, with the cost of debt denoted by $K_d$, we have that the expected return to debt holders is given by:

$$K_d = R_f + Risk\ Premium_d.$$

Notice that since equity holders face more ex ante risk than debt holders, and $R_f$ is the same for both equations, it follows that $Risk\ Premium_e > Risk\ Premium_d$ and hence $K_e > K_d$, reflecting equity holders' higher risk and associated higher expected return.

The expression for the combined expected return of both debt and equity holders is called the weighted average cost of capital (WACC), as

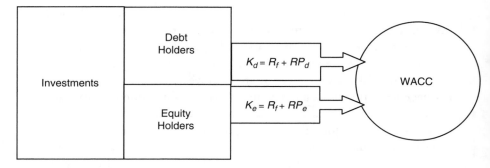

**Figure 1.5.** The Cost of Capital

the expected return is the firm's cost due to investors in exchange for receiving investment capital. WACC is computed as:

$$WACC = K_e \times \frac{E}{D+E} + K_d \times (1-t) \times \frac{D}{D+E},$$

where $K_e$ and $K_d$ are as defined previously, $E/(D+E)$ and $D/(D+E)$ are the weights that equity and debt contribute to finance the investment, and $t$ is the marginal income tax rate. Taxes enter the equation so as to allow us to compute the *after-tax* cost of capital. That is, since interest expenses can be deducted before determining taxable income, each dollar paid to the bank *saves t* dollars of taxes. As a result, the after-tax cost of debt is $K_d \times (1-t)$.

Figure 1.5 summarizes how we compute investors' combined expected return, or the cost of capital.

Managers tend to look carefully at the expected returns of their investors in an attempt to improve their ability to meet or beat (in the case of equity, only) these expectations. In the context of this book, which focuses on working capital management, we do not go further into the specific calculations necessary to determine each type of investor's risk premium, one of the most important and debated topics in corporate finance. Rather, we simply take risk premiums as a given, with the understanding that investors are willing to invest in exchange for a compensation that at least meets the minimum return required for the level of risk that investors face.

## CONCLUSION

In this introductory chapter, we presented a very simple framework of financial accounting, we introduced the two most basic financial statements, and we discussed their interaction. As a necessary complement, we also introduced the concepts of expected return and cost of capital.

We acknowledge that the discussion in this chapter has been deliberately light. As the purpose of this book is not to explain in full the mechanics of financial accounting but to shed light on working capital management, the discussion in this chapter is simply intended to review some of the key concepts that serve as a foundation for further analysis. More detailed discussion on these topics will be offered as necessary in the corresponding chapters of the book.

# 2

## Working Capital

Working capital is a complex concept. We have found, for example, that several managers and firm owners have difficulty when trying to go beyond its standard textbook definition to apply it to real-life situations. The reason behind such difficulty may be due to the apparent simplicity of the term: the standard definition, which states that working capital is obtained by deducting current liabilities from current assets, is so straightforward that one may not be guided to think very deeply about it. In reality, however, understanding only the explicit representation of the equation does not lead us very far toward the deeper understanding necessary for practitioners to correctly perform several standard corporate finance tasks.

This chapter develops a definition and interpretation of working capital that allows practitioners to use it correctly. In the first section, we begin by presenting the standard definition and interpretation. We then discuss why the standard definition alone fails to explain the whole story, and suggest that by introducing a second, complementary concept, namely, financial needs for operation, a more comprehensive understanding of working capital can be achieved. In the second section, we illustrate the mechanics of the interaction of working capital and financial needs for operation by way of a simple example. Finally, in the last two sections, we briefly analyze the factors that influence financial needs for operation and working capital; since we devote a complete chapter to the study of each of these factors, we discuss only their main features here.

## THE DEFINITION AND INTERPRETATION OF WORKING CAPITAL

So as to introduce a new term, Figure 2.1 presents a diagram of a balance sheet's various parts. As we can see from the figure, assets are divided into current and fixed assets, and liabilities are divided into short-term operating liabilities, long- and short-term financial debt, and equity.[1] Notice that *current liabilities* consist of short-term operating liabilities and short-term financial debt; long-term debt and equity are usually referred to as long-term capital.

With this in mind, working capital is usually defined as:

*Working Capital = Current Assets – Current Liabilities.*

This traditional definition of working capital shows how much cash (or liquid assets) is available to satisfy the short-term cash requirements imposed by current liabilities. Recall from Chapter 1 that accounting standards assume that an asset or a liability is a short-term item if it will be converted into cash (in the case of the assets) or become due (in the case of debts) within one year. Based on this assumption, current assets and current liabilities are usually considered short-term concepts. Thus, working capital is also commonly regarded as a short-term concept.

Figure 2.1 illustrates the intuition behind this definition of working capital using a very simple numerical example. The firm is assumed to have $500 in assets that will be converted into cash within one year, versus debts amounting to $400 that will become due within one year. The balance, equal to $100, is the standard measure of working capital.

Looking back at Figure 2.1, however, suggests that we can obtain an equivalent estimate of working capital by solving in the opposite direction, that is, by calculating working capital as:

*Working Capital = Capital $600 – Fixed Assets $500 = $100.*

Notice that we get the same numerical result using either approach, but when we use this alterative approach we do not find any short-term components in working capital, as capital and fixed assets are among the firm's most permanent and strategic components. Nevertheless, this second approach allows us to attain a different perspective, according to which working capital is the amount of capital that is devoted to financing the current assets of the firm.[2]

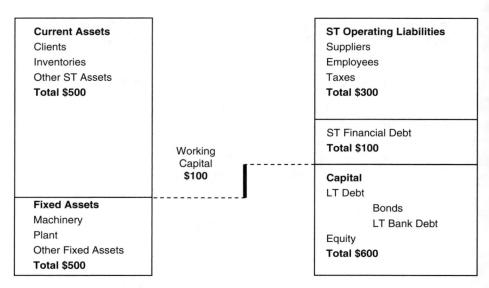

**Figure 2.1.** Working Capital

To complete our understanding of the definition of working capital, we need to back up a little bit and look at the intuition that in order to sustain its commercial activities, a firm needs to finance its operating investment. A firm's operating investment includes the firm's inventories (either raw materials or final goods), trade receivables, and a minimum level of liquidity so the company can operate normally—that is, the firm's current assets. This investment is usually financed in part by the firm's short-term *operating* liabilities, or the credits provided to the firm from suppliers, employees, and the tax authority. The firm's excess operating investment, which is the remaining financial capital needed to sustain the operation of the firm after taking into account its short-term operating liabilities, is referred to as its financial needs for operation (FNOs). Formally, FNOs are defined as:

*Financial Needs for Operation = Current Assets −*
*Short−term Operating Liabilities.*

Notice that short-term operating liabilities do not include short-term financial debts; rather, they are limited to debts with suppliers, employees, and the tax authority, debts that are generated spontaneously just by the mere fact of being in business.[3]

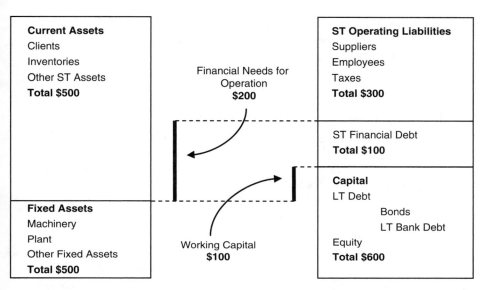

**Figure 2.2.** Financial Needs for Operation and Working Capital

Figure 2.2 adds FNOs to the example shown in Figure 2.1. In this example, the firm's FNOs are given by:

*Current Assets $500 – Short-term Operating Liabilities $300 = FNOs $200.*

Note that the firm's FNOs can be considered as a short-term concept, since both current assets and short-term operating liabilities vary with the firm's activity level and therefore with most of the tactical and short-term decisions of the company.

Since FNOs represent the *net* operating investment necessary to run the business, it is critical for a firm to find potential sources to finance this need. In figures 2.1 and 2.2, the firm in the example has partially covered its FNOs with working capital (which, viewed under our novel interpretation, is long-term finance) and thus has turned to the financial markets to close the gap between needs and sources of funds. Figure 2.2 shows that the difference is covered using short-term debt.

To summarize, we can say that the firm generates financial needs for operation. Working capital is one of the sources of funds the firm can use to finance that need; the balance will be financed using short-term financial debt. Under this framework, it is clear that the amount of working capital a firm decides to use is a strategic decision, as it determines how much of the FNOs to finance with long-term capital and how much to finance with short-term financial debt. In the next section of this chapter, we illustrate the importance of this strategic decision for firm performance and, in some cases, survival.

## A SIMPLE EXAMPLE

To help us obtain a better understanding of both financial needs for operation and working capital, we sketch a more detailed example. Imagine that John and Mary decide to start a new business, say, a pasta company. John will be in charge of marketing and sales, while Mary will be in charge of operations. Each of them buys 50% of the newly issued shares of the startup company for $100,000. The balance sheet of the firm after the company's first day is as depicted in Figure 2.3.

Before production can begin, the firm needs to acquire property in which to install a production facility. The firm also needs to obtain the necessary production and packaging equipment. We assume that the company pays $50,000 for the property and $150,000 for the equipment, financing these initial investments with cash obtained from the original equity issue. Figure 2.4 shows the balance sheet of the firm after setting up the production facility.

On the first day of operation, John obtains the company's first order: one of the largest grocery stores in town has placed an order for $10,000 in pasta. Since the firm will need to pay $5,000 for supplies and $4,000 for production costs (mostly to employees), the net profit of the sale, after deducting all the appropriate costs, will be $1,000. Mary contacts the supplier, buys the appropriate goods, and starts manufacturing the pasta. The supplier gives the new firm 60 days to pay the invoice, and employees will need to be paid in 30 days. However, John told Mary that the customer will pay the invoice

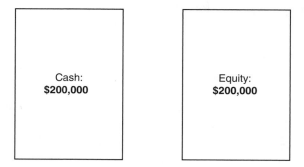

Cash:
**$200,000**

Equity:
**$200,000**

**Figure 2.3.** The Firm's Balance Sheet at Constitution

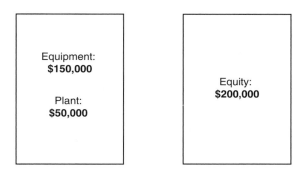

**Figure 2.4.** The Firm's Balance Sheet after the Initial Investments

in 60 days. After the first day of operation, the firm's balance sheet looks like that depicted in Figure 2.5.

Notice that the firm's equity has increased from $200,000 to $201,000. The difference represents the $1,000 profit arising from the sale.

At this point, it is useful to freeze the firm's operations and assume that nothing new happens so that we can analyze the financial effects of the first sale without receiving new information that might complicate our understanding of the dynamics at hand. After 30 days, employees need to be paid. The firm's balance sheet is as shown in Figure 2.6.

Note that the short-term financing provided by employees has now disappeared, as they need to be paid. But the firm faces a cash constraint: while it needs $4,000 to compensate employees, it does not have any liquid assets with which to make these payments. This cash constraint highlights the importance of the different maturities of assets and liabili-

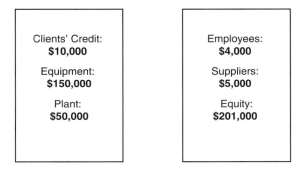

**Figure 2.5.** The Firm's Balance Sheet after the First Day of Operations

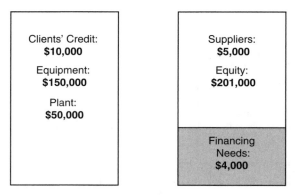

**Figure 2.6.** The Firm's Balance Sheet 30 Days after the First Sale

ties. In 30 more days the company would be able to resolve this issue, as that is when the customer will pay the firm the $10,000 owed. Meanwhile, however, the company needs $4,000 to stay alive until collection day.

At this point, we'll back up a little and summarize the financial history of the firm with an eye toward tracing the evolution of the firm's working capital. When John and Mary started the pasta company, their first set of investments was in property, plant, and equipment (PPE), which was entirely equity financed. At that stage, the company did not have any operating investment, and its working capital was equal to zero. With the first sale of pasta, the firm needed to make a second investment, as the grocery store buying their pasta needed financing of 60-day payment terms (i.e., payment of the $10,000 invoice was to be delayed for 60 days). This operational investment was initially financed by suppliers ($5,000), employees ($4,000), and the firm's profit share of the transaction ($1,000). At that point in time, the firm's FNOs amounted to $1,000 (i.e., current assets [$10,000] – short-term operating liabilities [$5,000 + $4,000]), and the firm's working capital was also equal to $1,000 (i.e., current assets [$10,000] – current liabilities [$9,000]).[4] After 30 days, however, the situation had changed; since the payment to employees became due, some of the short-term operating liabilities disappeared, the FNOs increased from $1,000 to $5,000 (i.e., current assets [$10,000] – suppliers [$5,000]), and working capital remained unchanged at $1,000. This caused a loss of balance between the firm's FNOs and working capital, requiring that the company find an additional source of financing to pay the $4,000 owed to employees.

Returning to our example, the timing mismatch between receipts and obligations is such that John and Mary need to obtain financing to bridge the gap. On the one hand, they can call a bank and ask for short-term financial debt. Alternatively, they can raise additional long-term capital, in the form of either long-term debt (by negotiating bank debt or issuing bonds) or equity (by issuing more equity). If they decide to raise more long-term capital, they would affect the level of working capital; in contrast, if they decide to issue short-term debt, working capital would remain unchanged. As a third option, the firm could try to obtain extra financing from suppliers and employees, which would have the effect of reducing the firm's FNOs.

The question of how to finance the firm's FNOs is one of management's most important strategic decisions. As we will see in Chapter 3, in order to make the best choice, management needs to have a very clear understanding of how the dynamics of FNOs work. We will see that FNOs usually react to increasing sales, which may result from sustainable growth or from seasonality.[5] Understanding the driver behind this change is crucial to choosing the optimal form of financing.

Obviously, the example presented in this chapter is extremely simplified. In the first place, John and Mary's pasta company was assumed to operate without inventory or cash holdings; each of these items, if they were to exist, would increase the firm's FNOs. Additionally, in the example the company does not face taxes; accrued taxes would reduce the firm's FNOs by increasing its short-term operating liabilities. Lastly, in this example we froze the firm's activity after the first transaction in an effort to better understand the mechanics of FNOs and working capital resulting from a single transaction. In real life, however, transactions are concatenated, with the gap between collections and corresponding payments harder to identify, mainly because of the continuous arrival of new information. Nonetheless, the workings of FNOs and working capital developed in this simplified example are identical to those that occur in real-life situations.

In the next section we will present a more comprehensive view on the dynamics and determinants of a firm's FNOs.

## DETERMINANTS OF FINANCIAL NEEDS FOR OPERATION

Recall that FNOs equal current assets minus short-term operating liabilities. This definition implies that any increase in current assets and/or decrease in short-term operating liabilities will result in an increase in a firm's FNOs; conversely, any decrease in current assets and/or increase in short-term operating liabilities will produce the opposite effect. Current assets mainly consist of customers' trade receivables, inventory, and cash holdings, while short-term operating liabilities consist of credits from suppliers, employees, and the tax authority.[6] Thus, it is clear that FNOs are closely related to the activity level of the firm. We will briefly discuss some of the main factors that influence FNOs in the following sections.

## Account Receivables

Companies often allow customers a specified number of days to pay their invoices. The use of such credits generates trade receivables, also known as account receivables. More specifically, goods or services delivered to customers on credit will increase the receivables balance, and payments subsequently received from customers will decrease this balance. Trade receivables thus show the balance of the *current account* that customers have with the firm on the balance date. On average, the balance of a given customer's current account is obtained by multiplying the daily volume of sales to that customer times the number of days the customer is allowed to take to pay the bill. If we extend this analysis to the whole firm, total account receivables is equal to the firm's average daily sales (i.e., total annual sales / 360) times the average collection period the firm sets across customers. More formally:

$$Account\ Receivables = Daily\ Sales \times Collection\ Period.$$

This equation shows that a firm's receivables are directly related to the level of the firm's sales and the number of days the firm allows its customers to take to pay their invoices. This implies that (1) as a firm grows in terms of sales, either because of sustained growth or seasonal growth, FNOs will increase, and (2) as the firm increases the collection period offered to its customers, FNOs will again increase.

Before moving on, we note that daily sales are a function of both sales volume and price. Therefore, we can say that:

$$Account\ Receivables = f\ (Sales\ Volume,\ Sales\ Price,\ Days\ Credit\ to\ Customers).$$

## Inventory

A firm's inventory is the necessary investment that the firm needs to make to ensure the normal operation of the business and a certain level of customer service. Some firms, because of their operating or commercial structure, need to make a large investment in inventory, while others can operate with a lower level of inventory. Usually, we can divide a firm's inventory into raw materials and finished goods.[7] When a company buys a unit of a given input, this is recorded in inventory at the purchase price, while when it produces a unit of a given product and stores it, this item is recorded in inventory according to its cost of goods sold. Firms usually define an optimal number of days to keep each kind of good in their inventory. The level of a firm's inventory at any point in time therefore reflects the total value of the goods kept by the firm, as measured by the goods' appropriate cost. On average, a firm's inventory balance can be calculated as follows:

$$Inventory = Daily\ Cost\ of\ Goods \times Days\ in\ Inventory.$$

Note that this equation masks a number of simplifications and shortcuts; we discuss this topic in greater detail in Chapter 6.[8] For our purposes here, however, this simple expression is useful in illustrating that a firm's inventory balance is a direct function of the cost of the goods held in inventory and the number of days that the goods are held in inventory. This implies that as either of these factors increases, FNOs also increase.

Similar to the case of receivables, we know that the daily cost of the goods held in inventory is a function of sales volume and the cost of buying or producing each good in question. Thus, we can say:

$$Inventory = f\ (Sales\ Volume,\ Cost\ of\ Goods,\ Days\ in\ Inventory).[9]$$

## Cash Holdings

Cash holdings are similar to inventory in that, to "keep the company going," management needs to be sure that the firm has a certain level of cash available to satisfy the cash requirements that arise during normal operations. Because the need for cash is usually associated with the firm's activity level and cash cycle, different firms are likely to establish different levels of cash holdings. In general terms, we can define cash holdings as a function of the firm's activity level, administrative efficiency, and production and cost structure. More formally:

$$Cash\ Holdings = f\ (Activity\ Level,\ Efficiency,\ Production,\ Cost\ Structure).$$

## Account Payables

Earlier in this section, we characterized customers' trade receivables; suppliers' trade credit works analogously. Suppliers sell their products to the firm and allow a certain amount of time before payment is due. Thus, account payables increases every time the firm receives a new shipment of goods and decreases every time it makes the corresponding payment. On average, the balance of one supplier's account is obtained by multiplying the daily volume of purchases from that supplier times the number of days the supplier allows before payment is due. If we extend this analysis to the whole firm, we can define account payables as the firm's average daily purchases times its average number of days of credit. More formally:

*Account Payables = Daily Purchases × Days Credit from Suppliers.*

Obviously, purchases are driven by sales. The determinants of suppliers' trade credit are thus sales volume, the price of raw materials, and days of credit:

*Account Payables = f (Units Bought, Price of the Goods, Days of Credit).*

As we mentioned, credit from employees and the tax authority add to the spontaneous resources of a firm, reducing the financial needs for operation.

To summarize, any increase in receivables, inventory, or cash holdings or any decrease in credit from suppliers, employees, or the tax authority will increase FNOs (and vice versa). It is worth pointing out, however, that most of these determinants are not always under the firm's control. For instance, while a firm might set a target level of sales growth, in reality, the firm's growth will be a function of factors such as the level of growth in the economy, the degree of competition in the market, and the level of advertising in the industry. Similarly, the ability to influence trade credit terms with customers or suppliers tends to vary over time according to the dynamics of the competitive environment and whether the firm enjoys a strong market power position (i.e., whether the firm is among the few suppliers of a given customer or among the few customers of a given supplier, in which case it would be easier for management to obtain favorable trade credit terms that decrease the firm's FNOs).

We cannot overstate the importance of the link between a firm's competitive position and ability to affect the level of FNOs to the dynamics of working capital management. Frequently, errors in corporate strategic and financial planning can be traced to the failure of management to recognize the link between strategy and working capital management.[10] In particular, managers' assumed levels of FNOs are usually overly optimistic. The upshot is that simple tools, such as Porter's analysis on the five competitive forces, can help prevent such errors.[11] In Chapter 3, we help shed more light on the mechanics of working capital management by studying the effects of seasonality and corporate growth on a firm's FNOs.

## DETERMINANTS OF WORKING CAPITAL

In contrast to FNOs, a firm strategically sets its level of working capital.[12] To maintain the desired level, the firm will need to adjust its capital structure over time. Notice that the working capital decision implies a choice with respect to the firm's financing: how much of the firm's current assets should the firm finance with long-term capital? A great deal of a treasurer's daily activity and a firm's future profitability is affected by this decision.

As we discussed earlier, a firm increases (decreases) its working capital when it increases (decreases) its level of equity or long-term debt and/ or when it decreases (increases) its level of fixed assets. Therefore, it is crucial to notice that decisions regarding fixed assets and long-term debt and equity are decisions over how to set the appropriate level of working capital. Consequently, working capital should not be considered simply a short-term decision, nor should it be revised or determined solely on a short-term, or operating, basis.

## CONCLUSION

In this chapter, we showed that in order to correctly understand the mechanics and implications of a firm's working capital, we need to take into account a firm's financial needs for operation, or FNOs. A firm's FNOs are the level of operating investment needed for the company to operate its business. This investment can be financed using working capital and/or short-term financial debt. Because a firm's working capital and FNOs are interconnected, use of only one of them in isolation will usually lead the manager astray. Indeed, decisions regarding the mix of working capital and short-term financial debt are among the firm's important strategic, or long-term, business decisions. In the next chapter, we look at how these should be combined along a firm's dynamic path.

# 3

## Working Capital, Seasonality, and Growth

The connection between a given level of operating activity and the choice of working capital is oftentimes misunderstood. In turn, the selection of optimal financing is often incorrect, which, depending on the specific economic environment, can lead to a small loss, a significant reduction of business profitability, or even total lack of viability of the firm.[1] The goal of this chapter is to help managers better understand the relation between a firm's level of operating activity and working capital. Firms tend to match financing maturity with their assets' average life.[2] This may lead the manager to finance short-term operating assets with short-term debt. However, such a practice would ignore the fact that a certain portion of short-term operating assets resembles fixed assets. To explore this intuition, let's assume that a company has a 90-day collection period. The firm can expect to collect current receivables within three months. Of course, as long as the company continues operating and generating new sales, it will replace the current receivables with new ones. Thus, while *certain* receivables will disappear, the firm will always have *some*! In turn, while trade receivables may be individually considered short-term assets, taken as a class, they last longer than most fixed assets (which typically get depreciated).

So, how should a firm think about financing its operation? This whole process typically starts with a more or less detailed analysis of corporate strategy, expected demand for the firm's products, associated production costs, trade credit and inventory policies, and so forth. The inputs are, in most cases, determined outside the finance department. The CFO, however, needs to collaborate with operating managers, mainly to warn about potential restrictions on commercial, operational, and similar types of policies, and suggest solutions to the firm. Once all of these elements are collected, the CFO is ready to build the financial plan for the near future, which starts by defining external financial needs and continues by designing the appropriate way of satisfying them.

In this chapter, we address the question of how a firm should finance its operation by taking a close look at the financing choices available to the firm, the criteria for the optimal selection among them, and the influence of seasonality and growth over the particular choice.

## THE EFFECTS OF SEASONALITY ON WORKING CAPITAL

Many industries are characterized by high seasonality. A seasonal business is one in which the majority of its trade occurs during a short period each year, or a business that experiences substantial changes in trading activity throughout the year. Typical examples of seasonal businesses are those operating in the toy, tourism, and farming industries. For these businesses, it is essential to consider the impact of seasonality on the optimal level of working capital.

Recall that a firm's net operating investment (or financial needs for operation [FNOs]) consists of cash (necessary to more or less cover immediate operating expenses), account receivables or credit to customers, and inventories, and it is naturally estimated as net of financing obtained from suppliers (i.e., account payables). One might expect the impact of seasonality on a firm's operating activity to be such that, during the seasonal peak, the firm will require higher net investment in short-term (current) assets and therefore higher working capital. This intuition, however, is part of the usual confusion.

To see this, let's consider the case of a firm whose main activity is the production and sale of toys (the toy industry is highly seasonal, with most of its sales concentrated between October and December). What happens to the operating investment of the toy company during its seasonal peak? To answer this question, let's look at each of the components of operating investment. First, would it have more cash on its balance sheet? Probably yes, since it is likely that the firm will face higher costs, such as production and marketing costs, during this time. Second, would the firm maintain higher levels of inventory in its balance sheet during the high season? Presumably. The timing for the increase in inventory will depend on whether the firm selects a *level* production plan, which has a stable production rate, or a *seasonal* production plan, where production follows sales, but in either case average inventory will generally be higher during the peak season.[3] Third, would the firm show greater account receivables during the peak? Certainly. To help fund this higher operating investment, the firm will likely rely on more financing from suppliers. Nevertheless, the firm's net operating investment (i.e., FNOs) is likely to be higher during the peak season. But does it follow that the firm will consequently require higher working capital?

Let's go back to our basic concepts. Recall from Chapter 2 that FNOs are a short-term financing notion, whereas working capital is mostly connected to long-term finance.[4] This became obvious when we departed from the traditional *accounting* view of working capital (i.e., current assets minus current liabilities) and defined it as the difference between the permanent resources and the fixed (noncurrent) assets of the firm. We illustrate the connection between these concepts once more in Figure 3.1.

Now, let's use this new perspective to analyze what happens to working capital when the toy company enters its peak season. Will the manager be likely to finance the firm's higher operating activity by increasing the working capital *invested* in the firm? Well, let's think! Will the toy producer issue new long-term debt, or even equity, in order to finance increased activity during these three months? Considering the related issuance, agency, and information costs, this would probably be an inefficient solution.[5] As a consequence (under the conditions we are exploring right now), the firm's *permanent resources* will probably remain unchanged throughout the year. What about the firm's fixed assets (which affect working capital in the opposite direction)? Will our toy producer

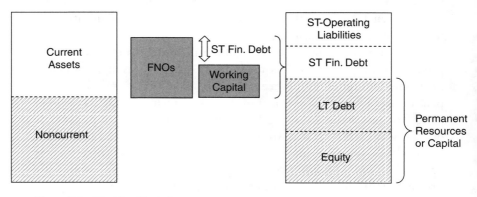

**Figure 3.1.** Working Capital

be likely to, say, buy a new truck to adjust her distribution system according to the high season's requirements? If she does, she would have to sell it back right after the high season ends to avoid an increase in idle capacity! So this does not sound like a reasonable strategy either; that is, *noncurrent assets* are also likely to remain unchanged. So if permanent resources (long-term debt and equity) do not change, and noncurrent assets do not change, working capital, by construction, cannot change. Ergo, seasonality should not affect decisions about the optimal level of working capital.

The previous discussion sounds like a proof. However, it does not silence our perceptions, which tell us that *something* changes during seasonal peaks. If working capital does not change, what does? The answer: the firm's FNOs.

Let's imagine the summarized accounting information presented in Table 3.1, which corresponds to a period of low activity. At the current activity level, the firm's FNOs are equal to $600; that is, it has to look for that amount of funds. Now imagine that the firm's high season arrives, during which time sales are 50% higher; assume operating ratios remain the same. What will the firm's new FNOs be? In Figure 3.2, we observe that when the activity level changes—due, in this case, to a seasonal peak—the financial needs for operation also change; if operating ratios remain constant, they change proportionally.

At this stage, our simple example leads us to the following conclusion: when a firm faces seasonal changes in its trading activity, the firm's working capital should remain the same throughout the year but its FNOs should vary with the level of trading activity. In other words, as the firm increases its activity level, its FNOs should follow the trend; however, because the higher level of activity is expected to last only *temporarily*, the firm has no incentive to change its working capital (which should change as a result of long-term changes in business activity). Graphically, we can summarize this conclusion as shown in Figure 3.3.

Table 3.1. Baseline

| | |
|---|---|
| Sales | $1,000 |
| Cash | $100 |
| Account Receivables | $600 |
| Inventory | $400 |
| Account Payables | $500 |
| **FNOs** | **$600** |

| Sales | $ 1,000 | | Sales | $ 1,500 |
|---|---|---|---|---|

+ 50%

| Cash | $ 100 | | Cash | $ 150 |
|---|---|---|---|---|
| Account Receivables | $ 600 | | Account Receivables | $ 900 |
| Inventory | $ 400 | | Inventory | $ 600 |
| Account Payables | $ 500 | | Account Payables | $ 750 |

| FNOs | $ 600 | + 50% | FNOs | $ 900 |
|---|---|---|---|---|

**Figure 3.2.** 50% Growth

We now have the question: if during its high season the firm increases its net operating investment (i.e., FNOs) but does not change its long-term financing, how does the firm cover the gap? Again, we turn to Chapter 2 for insight. In Chapter 2, we learned that, following the conceptual path, we should estimate FNOs as the difference between current assets and spontaneous resources, but we can also compute them as the sum of short-term debt and working capital. This second expression makes it clear that the necessary net operating investment can be financed in two possible ways: working capital or short-term debt, where working capital is interpreted not simply as an investment decision but also as a financing strategy. In our previous graphs, we can see that whatever is not covered with working capital is financed with short-term debt.

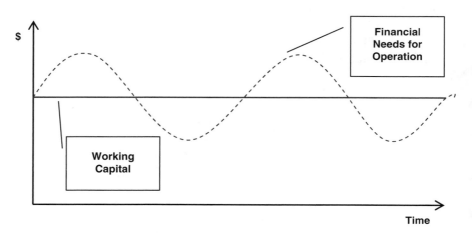

**Figure 3.3.** Fluctuations

This discussion suggests that when a firm faces seasonality, it needs to analyze how to mix alternative sources of funding in order to cover financing needs that vary over time. To deepen our analysis, we now explore alternative financing strategies.

Imagine that the firm's manager wants to minimize raising long-term financing to avoid having to pay associated fees on funds that are not needed during long periods of lower activity. In this case, the manager picks a level of working capital equal to the minimum monthly operating financial need and covers all peaks with short-term financing. Figure 3.4 illustrates this choice. The graph shows that during the high season, the firm will increase its operating investment and, since working capital does not change, the increased investment will be financed using short-term financial debt. During the low season, in contrast, the firm covers all its financial needs with working capital and has zero short-term financing.

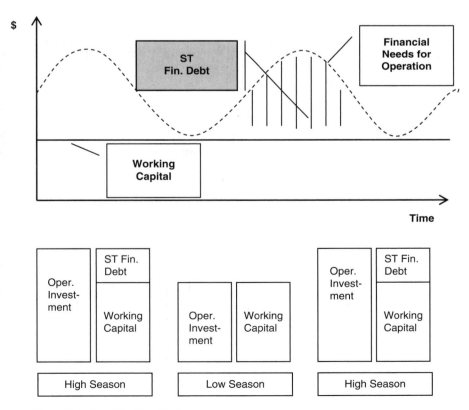

**Figure 3.4.** Low Working Capital

Under *normal* conditions, this strategy could be a cheap one: it minimizes the use of more expensive long-term capital.[6] However, in a more risky or uncertain market environment, this strategy could subject the firm to a high level of risk. For example, if, when the firm's financing requirement is high, a credit crunch or a similar crisis makes it impossible to raise short-term financing, this strategy could lead the firm to miss out on participating in the hot market and in turn to suffer a considerable loss or even bankruptcy. Additionally, strategies like this one entail high interest rate risk: since the average permanent investment is higher than this minimum level for which the firm has chosen long-term finance (i.e., working capital), there would be a mismatch between the average life of the assets and their corresponding financing source.

Now imagine that the manager decides to pursue the opposite strategy. That is, to avoid rushing in search of immediate financing for each peak, she chooses a high level of working capital covered by long-term finance. This extreme scenario is depicted in Figure 3.5.

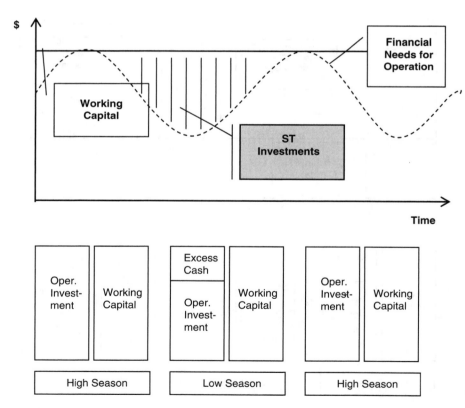

**Figure 3.5.** High Working Capital

Following this second strategy, the manager could sleep very confidently, knowing that all her *potential* operating financials needs will be covered. However, her comfortable *pillow* is likely to be extremely expensive, with the firm not using its assets to their full potential. During low season, there would be more funds than necessary within the firm (i.e., idle funds), which, being long-term loans or even equity, are likely to require a considerable return. The idle funds could certainly be invested in short-term assets (so that they would be easily available whenever needed), but the return on such investments is generally low, particularly if one compares it with its associated cost. Moreover, this strategy also implies assuming some interest rate risk. Since the duration of assets would be, on average, shorter than the duration of liabilities, interest rate variation would break the balance among them. For example, if the economy enters a recession, leading to lower interest rates, even though the value of both assets and liabilities would increase, the latter would do so more strongly, weakening the financial position of the firm.[7]

Which of these strategies is the best one to follow? The answer probably depends, among other things, on the business's debt capacity and its access to debt. A firm's location is also likely to influence this decision: if the seasonal firm is in the United States, Germany, or similar countries (where financing opportunities are usually relatively easy to access), the optimal choice would probably require a lower investment in working capital (long-term operating finance) than if the same business were located in a developing country (which typically has less deep/liquid financial and capital markets and frequently experiences credit-crunch phenomena). However, in general, the optimal strategy is not likely to be characterized by either of these extreme strategies, but rather is likely to lie somewhere in between. Such an intermediate strategy is depicted in Figure 3.6.

The trade-off between the goals of minimizing low-return investments (*idle* cash) and avoiding liquidity risk should guide the proper level of working capital selected. Given this choice, the portion of financial needs for operation that are not covered with working capital will be financed with short-term debt. Thus, while a sound financial policy will count on long-term financing to partially cover varying financial needs, short-term debt should be optimally raised to finance seasonal cash shortages due to changes in operational investment.

When firms fail to have a coherent working capital policy in the context of a developed capital market, a wise advisor would probably point that out and the firm would correct the problem, experiencing almost no frictions. When the firm instead operates in an emerging economy, which, as we've noted, usually have low-quality capital markets (i.e., capi-

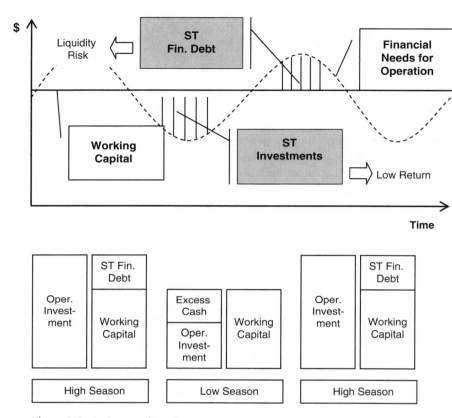

**Figure 3.6.** An Intermediate Case

tal is in short supply, market size and liquidity are an issue, and institutional failures are common), inappropriate financing of operating activities can lead the firm into financial distress.

### FINANCING GROWTH

So far, we have considered the problem of a manager selecting the optimal level of working capital for the case of firms facing seasonality. However, this optimal decision is potentially, indeed, most likely, dynamic: most firms not only observe seasonal variation in economic activity but also grow over time. For example, firms that belong to non-mature industries may experience growth as a part of the natural process, while firms in more mature industries may pursue growing strategies based on market power contests or acquisition plans. Of course, not all businesses experience positive growth—there are businesses that decrease over time, either due to their own decisions or as a consequence of shocks to the economic environment. The question we turn to here is whether a firm should adjust its working capital when it experiences not just seasonality but also a clearly defined trend (either positive or negative) in activity level.

Let's think of a firm that has been following a growth strategy over the last four or five years. We can imagine that the growth pattern is not even, but rather can be characterized by swings resulting from implementing programs suggested by the firm's various departments. For example, the commercial manager may have suggested that the firm encourage sales by giving customers longer payment periods (i.e., by increasing the collection period) at the same time that the operations department recommended increasing inventory (quantity and variety) in order to provide better service.[8] These measures would effectively increase the amount invested in current assets (specifically, account receivables and inventory), even if the firm were supposed to continue operating at the same activity level (certainly, managers are expecting this not to continue to be the case—they are offering strategies precisely to increase sales—but let's go step by step).

Imagine a firm that, without changing any commercial, production, or operational policy, is experiencing a sudden increase in sales (e.g., consumers started going crazy about one of its key products). Since the investment in, say, receivables will be equal to *number of days of customers' credit × daily sales,* the firm's operational investment will certainly be higher. We already saw this in the previous chapter.

However, the impact of growth on operational investment will be stressed if it results not only from an external phenomenon (such as fashion hits or general market growth) but also from the firm's strategic decisions. That is, if the firm takes actions that extend its operating ratios (days of receivables or inventory) in order to increase sales, operating investment will grow not only due to simple higher daily volume but also because each dollar of sales requires higher operating investment.

As an example, consider a firm that used to allow customers to pay in 15 days, but that has extended the collection period to 20 days, thereby attracting more customers and in turn increasing sales.[9] For each dollar of sales, there would now be five extra days of account receivables waiting to be cashed in. There would also be more sales dollars to finance. This represents a supplementary investment in customers equal to *5 days × the previous daily volume + 20 days × the volume increase in daily sales.* In this case, both the increase in the collection period and the higher level of sales would require higher investment in current assets, investment that would require additional financing. This type of strategy is depicted in Figure 3.7.

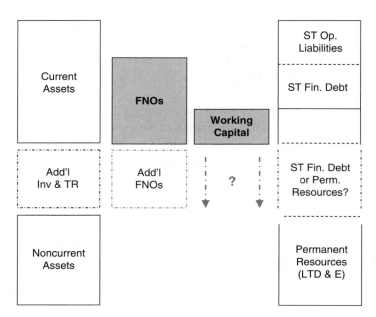

**Figure 3.7.** Financing the Gap

Given that the firm must increase its investment in current assets to implement its strategic growth policies, the firm has to choose between financing this investment with short-term debt or working capital. But how should this decision be made? Is it optimal, as in the case of a seasonal firm, to maintain a given level of working capital and cover all additional financing requirements with short-term debt? Let's explore this option. If the firm decides to maintain its level of working capital, the situation would be as depicted in Figure 3.8.

As we can see from the figure, the gap between the financial needs for operation and the corresponding long-term financing (working capital) would increase over time. Ergo, the firm would need even greater access to credit (short-term debt), which is not always available—particularly in the case of emerging markets. As a consequence, the company will be able to take advantage of all possible growth opportunities only in those cases in which the current financial market climate makes it possible to access the necessary funds. This is a very risky strategy.

Most firms would instead choose a level of working capital that moves in response not to seasonal sales variation, but to a well-defined trend in the level of economic activity (which is indicated with a dashed line in Figure 3.8). The shape of the adjustment path will depend on firm and market characteristics. One possible scenario is shown in Figure 3.9.

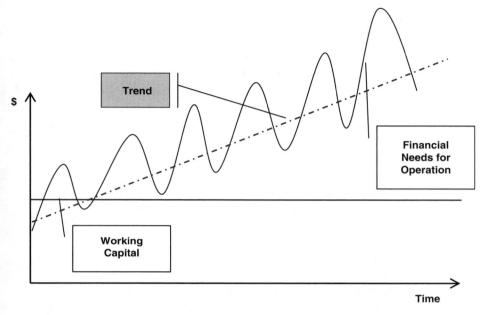

**Figure 3.8.** Financing Growth

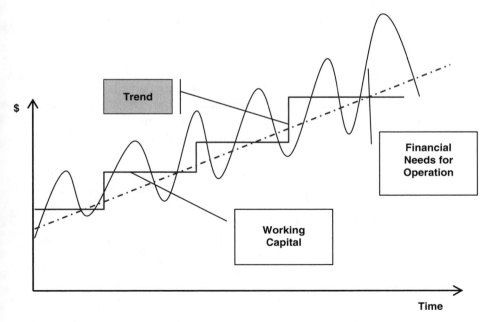

**Figure 3.9.** Financing Growth

## POSITIVE VERSUS NEGATIVE WORKING CAPITAL STRATEGIES AND GROWTH

Earlier, we showed that a pattern of increased trading activity normally requires greater investment in working capital. However, while this is quite intuitive, it is true only under certain assumptions—there are both industries and firms that, based on some particular market condition or corporate strategy, tend to perform differently. We now analyze some cases in which this relation may not apply.

Consider first the investment in current assets of airlines. These firms' sales are typically made on the basis of cash or short-term credit card financing; on average, they have a collection period (i.e., account receivables) of less than 15 days. Moreover, outstanding inventory also tends to be low (as is the case for most service businesses); let's pick a 10-day ratio. Finally, especially in the case of large airlines, which enjoy market power, suppliers often provide between 20 and 30 days of financing. The FNOs of airlines are therefore close to zero or even negative, which implies that these firms are able to pursue a self-financing growth strategy.

Next, consider businesses in which inventory of high turnover or perishable goods is normally delivered at high-frequency intervals (e.g., on a daily basis). The use of automatic replenishment systems, together with the effective exercise of market power, allows these firms to maintain relatively low levels of inventory; let's pick for our example a holding period of about seven days. What about trade receivables? Even though some fraction of sales is made on credit, the regular collection period is fairly short, probably less than 10 days. Turning to financing from suppliers, given the volume and consequent market power characterizing some of these businesses (e.g., McDonalds), we can assume a pretty long payment period. Taken together, and considering that these firms will likely have a few days' cash on hand, we again have a class of firms that are likely to have zero or negative FNOs, that is, companies that are capable of self-financing their growth.

Note that zero or negative FNOs may arise not just from patterns particular to a firm's industry but also from a specific firm's business strategy—a strategy that may even break industry patterns. A classic example is the case of Dell. Dell's strategy consists of providing online-based, customized sales, which translates into almost zero inventory and accounts receivable: Dell's customers place their order on the internet, together with their credit card information; only after payment information has been processed does the firm inform its suppliers to start building the required system. This strategy, as has been widely documented, allowed Dell to grow steadily without requiring high investment in working capital.

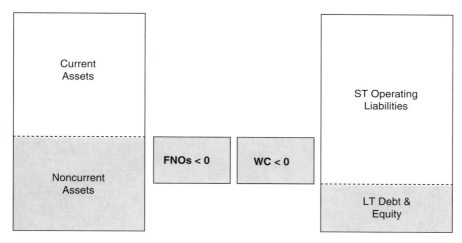

**Figure 3.10.** Negative Financial Needs for Operation

It is instructive at this point to stop to reflect again on the differ-ences—and complementarities—between FNOs and working capital. In this section so far, we are *not* focusing attention on firms or industries that are distinguished for simply having *negative working capital* (although these firms would indeed have negative working capital). Rather, we are pointing out that firms that have low required investment in current assets (because of industry patterns or a particular business strategy) and that are likely to rely on significant financing from suppliers experience *negative FNOs*. Moreover, we are saying that, under these conditions, a firm is likely to be able to self-finance its operations and hence would not need to search for financing (be it short-term debt or working capital), regardless of whether the firm faces seasonality or pursues steady growth. Figure 3.10 shows this graphically.

Note that in the previous scenario, a firm's working capital will not always be equal to its FNOs (as it appears in Figure 3.10). Indeed, this would be the case only if short-term debt were equal to zero. In contrast, if there is at least some short-term debt, working capital will be larger (in absolute value) than the FNOs.

Shifting gears, we now consider a totally different scenario, namely, one in which a firm has *positive* FNOs (i.e., a positive financing gap) and negative working capital.[10] This scenario is depicted in Figure 3.11.

In this case, the firm needs to *actively* finance its operation (i.e., FNOs are greater than zero), and it does so completely with short-term finance. Note that the short-term finance even covers part of the firm's fixed

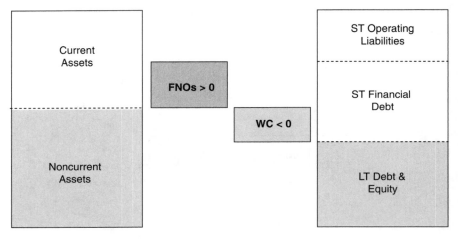

**Figure 3.11.** Negative Working Capital

investment. In general, this is very risky: the firm doesn't simply fail to finance long-term investment with long-term sources of funds (either debt or equity), but it sustains the whole operation (which, as we have observed, is not completely short term in *real terms*) with short-term financing. What could be potential reasons for doing this? Perhaps the firm has a particular view about future business conditions, or more likely it has no other option (i.e., it faces financing constraints). Indeed, it is often the case in emerging economies that firms are unable to match asset and liability maturities due to market restrictions—they get the financing they *can*. We will go over these issues later, when we discuss working capital management in the context of emerging markets.

## CONCLUSION

The punch line of this analysis is that, while revenues (cash flow) should be financed with short-term debt, profits (growth) should be financed with more permanent sources. Put differently, while seasonality-related sales should be funded primarily through the use of short-term financing, growth should be funded by adjusting the level of working capital—with the exception of firms and/or industries that enjoy low required investment in current assets and high supplier financing, that is, negative FNOs and working capital. This distinction in optimal funding for seasonality and growth should have clear implications for a company's financial planning. In particular, failure to differentiate between seasonal fluctuations in economic activity and actual growth will cause the firm to either take suboptimal financing risks (financing with short-term debt investments that really call for long-term financing, resulting in the risk that some opportunities may not receive funding) or pay too high a required return on financial capital (financing short-term needs with long-term debt, resulting in idle funds upon which payments are due).

# 4

## Financial Analysis and Working Capital

It is not easy to draw many conclusions about a firm's performance or prospects just by inspecting the main financial statements that the firm generates, as reported numbers are influenced by many factors such as a firm's size, technology, industry, and country. However, the information contained in financial statements can be reorganized into ratios that, combining absolute numbers, can shed some light on the financial conditions of the firm. For instance, these ratios can be used to analyze the evolution of a firm over time or to evaluate the firm's performance against that prevailing in the industry.

To correctly interpret the information contained in a ratio, it is key to understand how it has been built. Most ratios are conventions that change slightly from user to user, according to preferences, custom, and experience. However, since each ratio is a tool that helps us answer a particular question, and given that most people conducting financial analysis tend to ask similar questions, there are a set of "traditional" or "popular" ratios that are fairly standardized. These ratios can be classified into four broad categories according to the type of question they address; in particular, we can organize a firm's financial statement information into ratios to examine the firm's profitability, liquidity, operating efficiency, and financial leverage.

In this chapter, we begin by introducing the most commonly used ratios, according to these four broad categories. In particular, we analyze their construction and interpretation. Next, we consider some other ratios, based on market data. Finally, we discuss how comprehensive analysis of these ratios can shed light on a firm's working capital management practices and expected prospects.

## FINANCIAL RATIOS

In this section, we describe the construction and interpretation of the primary ratios used to summarize firms' financial information. After introducing these key ratios, we consider how they can be used to convey information about a firm's condition or to forecast a firm's future prospects.

### Profitability Ratios

Business profitability is among a manager's main concerns (except, perhaps, for managers of nonprofits). Given that the concept of profitability is broad, it is critical that one determines both the accounting level at which profits are measured and the scale factor used in their calculation. For example, with respect to level data, in some instances it may be useful to evaluate a firm's operating profits by comparing them to those of similar businesses regardless of leverage considerations (i.e., measuring profits at the earnings before interest and taxes level, either before deducting amortization [EBITDA] or after [EBIT]), whereas in other instances one may like to focus on the bottom line, that is, on net income. With respect to scaling factors, they can vary from net sales or assets, in the former case, to equity investment, in the latter case. The important thing about scaling factors when building ratios is that numerators and denominators correspond to the same claim holders.

One of the most commonly used profitability indexes is *return on equity* (ROE), which is typically computed as the ratio between net income and equity investment:

$$ROE = \frac{Net\ Income}{Equity}.$$

This ratio provides an accounting measure of shareholders' profitability (i.e., how much shareholders get for each dollar invested in the firm). However, as we will see is the case with most accounting ratios, ROE is sensitive to specific reporting criteria and thus the calculated ratio may differ from the underlying economic reality. For example, ROE uses book value of equity as its denominator, which usually deviates from a market value perspective. That is, it is highly likely that a firm's ROE does not correspond exactly to the actual return on the capital that shareholders invest in the firm. Nonetheless, the ratio is widely used.

It is important to notice that ROE takes into account the effects of financial leverage on net profit; in other words, given that profits are being measured *after* accounting for the corresponding interest expenses, two firms with different capital structures that are otherwise identical will present different ROE given their different leverage choices. We will return to this topic later in this section, in the discussion on the most widely used leverage ratios.

Turning to the next ratio of interest, when managers want to concentrate on business profitability without considering the effects of leverage, they typically use a figure based on EBIT. Given that EBIT refers to profits that should be distributed to both creditors and shareholders, the corresponding scaling factor should not be shareholders' equity but rather assets (again, numerators and denominators need to correspond to the same claim holders). Therefore, this index is typically computed as:

$$ROA = \frac{EBIT}{Total\ Assets},$$

where ROA equals return on assets. Going deeper into this analysis, one might recall that, as discussed in Chapter 2, a portion of total assets may be financed by suppliers, who do not charge explicit financing costs but build compensation for this service into the price they charge for their products. Thus, a manager may wish to measure profitability over the *net* investment made by debt and equity holders. Accordingly, it has become customary to modify the previous ratio by using *net assets* instead of total assets as the scaling factor. Net assets can be thought of as the net investment (both current and noncurrent) that is financed by sources of funds that claim an explicit financial return (i.e., total assets minus account payables and other current liabilities that do not present explicit costs, such as accrued taxes or pending labor expenses). Thus, using net assets as the scaling factor, we have:

$$RONA = \frac{EBIT}{Net\ Assets},$$

where RONA equals return on net assets. Notice, however, that EBIT is to be distributed across debt holders, equity holders, and the fiscal authority, while net assets are financed only by debt and equity holders. This violates the required congruence between the ratios' numerators and denominators. To solve this problem, we simply modify the previous RONA as follows:

$$RONA = \frac{EBIT \times (1-t)}{Net\ Assets}.$$

In the modified RONA, the expression $(1 - t)$ suggests that the tax authority's share of the firm's gross profit is equal to $t$; that is, the company has no leverage-generated tax shield.[1] In reality, this is unlikely to be the case. However, the previous definition provides a general measure of return that is not influenced by leverage considerations. The impact of a company's actual tax shield will be considered in the required return this figure will often be compared to.[2]

The last so-called profitability ratios that we introduce here are typically based on sales and/or some combination of different revenue items taken from the income statement. The most common such ratios are:

$$\frac{Net\ Income}{Sales} \quad and\ /\ or \quad \frac{EBITDA}{Sales}.$$

These ratios are not real profitability ratios. First, they stress the concept of *margin,* which, as we will discuss later in this chapter, is only one of the components of profitability. Moreover, these ratios are generally used to compare a firm's efficiency and/or business strategy against other comparable firms or against the whole industry, and thus they should really be considered among the operating (efficiency) ratios presented later in this chapter.[3]

Before moving on to discuss the next class of ratios, we would like to emphasize that some managers tend to use profitability ratios that do not make real financial sense, for example, Net Profit / Total Assets or EBIT / Equity. These ratios show inconsistency between the numerator and the denominator (i.e., between who gets the profit and who makes the investment). It is therefore important that an analyst carefully consider how a given ratio has been constructed in evaluating the information content of the ratio.

### Liquidity Ratios

We begin our discussion of liquidity ratios with a discussion of what "liquidity" means. A liquid asset is typically characterized as an asset that is easily converted into cash. But what does this mean? The conversion-to-cash characterization typically implies three conditions. First, it implies that the asset can be converted into cash in a short period of time. But this condition is not sufficient to describe liquidity. To see this, consider a firm's property, plant, and equipment (PPE). While PPE is usually considered illiquid, a manager could convert the firm's PPE into cash quickly if he or she were ready to accept a considerable price discount. Thus, the conversion-to-cash characterization also implies that the conversion can be effected without significant loss of value. A third, and recently recognized, condition of liquidity is that the asset be *scalable,* that is, that any given quantity of the asset can be converted into cash.[4]

So, we have that a liquid asset is one in which we can quickly convert any amount of the asset into cash without much loss of value. But why do we care about liquidity? Liquidity analysis helps one determine whether the firm would be able to pay off its debts as they become due over a one-year period (remember that one condition of liquidity is connected to speed; we are thus talking about the short run). One way to address such a question would be to investigate firms' commercial policies and their impact on accessing cash. However, by comparing current assets, which by definition could be transformed into cash within a year, with current liabilities, which are due also within a one-year period, one can more easily assess the company's general ability to cover its short-term debts. This ratio, which is called the *liquidity ratio,* indicates how many dollars a firm will be able to get in the short run for each dollar that it needs to pay in the same time horizon, where convention usually defines the short run to be one year. More formally, this ratio is given as:

$$Liquidity\ Ratio = \frac{Current\ Assets}{Current\ Liabilities}.$$

Note that in the case of this ratio and most of the ratios we discuss later in this chapter, there is no "right number." The ratio is just an indicator that can be compared with the firm's past information or with a benchmark of comparable firms. If, for example, one finds that a firm's liquidity ratio has decreased over time (or that, at one point in time, it is smaller than the liquidity ratios of industry peers), one would then need to analyze whether this is good news or bad news with respect to the firm's prospects. To make such a determination requires that one conduct a more comprehensive examination of the firm. We turn to a discussion of such analysis later in this chapter.

Another common measure of liquidity is the *quick ratio,* which is more restrictive than the previous measure. Specifically, given that in some industries inventory is less liquid than other types of current assets, this measure excludes inventory from the pool of liquid assets. The expression for this ratio is thus formulated as:

$$Quick\ Ratio = \frac{Current\ Assets - Inventories}{Current\ Liabilities}.$$

The relevance of using the quick ratio versus the more general liquidity ratio depends on the actual liquidity of a firm's inventory. For example, the quick ratios of grocery stores would be almost meaningless, given the high liquidity of their inventory, whereas the quick ratios of producers of durable goods would permit the evaluation of the real possibility of paying off short-term liabilities without having to sell illiquid inventory (most likely at a loss).

An additional liquidity indicator can be obtained by measuring *days of cash,* which gives the number of days a firm would be able to cover all its expenses with the cash (or cashlike assets) it has on hand. This indicator can be calculated as follows:

$$Days\ of\ Cash = \frac{Cash\ and\ Marketable\ Securities}{Daily\ Expenses}.$$

It is worth noting that this ratio combines a *flow variable* (which corresponds to a period of time), taken from the income statement, with a *stock* variable (which corresponds to a moment in time), taken from the balance sheet. Consequently, we need to be careful about factors such as seasonality that may affect the figures reported in the balance sheet, and the length of time considered in the income statement.

For instance, if we are analyzing a seasonal business, the figures reported in the balance sheet may not represent the average life of the business. Consider a fireworks producer; we would expect balance sheet figures in June to be totally different from what they would be in December, as the cash balances that the firm will choose to maintain to cover payments due during the peak are likely to be larger than what they would be during the off-season. Consequently, days of cash would be more appropriately estimated by averaging information from, say, quarterly statements.

Turning to the time period considered, while the flow variables in the income statement typically correspond to annual, quarterly, or monthly periods, the days-of-cash ratio provides a measure based in days. Hence, the information taken from the income statement has to be converted into days to calculate the ratio correctly. If we are using annual statements, for example, daily expenses are estimated by dividing the corresponding accounts (which normally include all expenses minus those not representing actual payments, such as amortization, depreciation, and provisions) by 360.[5] If we are using monthly statements, the figures are divided by 30. And so on.

A related issue arises from the implicit assumption that days-of-cash and similar ratios make about the pace at which flow variables *flow*. Specifically, while *days of cash* assumes that payments are made homogeneously (smoothly) throughout the period considered in the income statement, this may not always be the case. Again, if we are managing a seasonal business, expenses may be concentrated over a period of time that is much shorter than the reference period, so that the interpretation of the ratio may need to be adjusted.

### Operating (Efficiency) Ratios

Operating ratios focus on the efficiency with which a firm administers its assets; in other words, they summarize information that helps one assess whether a firm is investing the right amount in each type of operating asset. As with most other ratios, the exact calculation of these indicators varies across firms and industries. Also as before, the figures generated by this class of ratios do not need to match any particular accounting number; rather, it is the differences over time or across firms that are of interest, as such differences point to the quality of the firm's underlying business conditions and/or strategic decisions.

The key operating ratios are *days of receivables, days of inventory,* and *days of payables.* Their formulation can be summarized as:

$$Days \ of \ Receivables = \frac{Account \ Receivables}{Daily \ Sales}$$

$$Days \ of \ Inventory = \frac{Inventory}{Daily \ Cost \ of \ Goods \ Sold}$$

$$Days \ of \ Payables = \frac{Account \ Payables}{Daily \ Purchases}.$$

*Days of receivables* represents the number of days before a company receives payment on its sales. *Days of inventory* gives the number of days the firm can keep selling without producing new goods or buying merchandise. *Days of payables* represents the number of days a firm can take before paying its commercial obligations.

A set of closely related ratios consists of *inventory turnover* and *asset turnover*:

$$Inventory\, Turnover = \frac{Sales}{Inventory}$$

$$Asset\, Turnover = \frac{Sales}{Assets}.$$

In a strict sense, these ratios represent how many times a company sells its inventory or assets, respectively. For example, a small inventory turnover ratio (i.e., a figure that is much smaller than it used to be or smaller than the industry average) would imply that there is excessive inventory in the firm for the current level of sales or, in other words, that there is unproductive investment (i.e., inventory balances that are not generating sales).[6] Similarly, the asset turnover ratio shows the efficiency with which not only inventory but also equipment and other fixed investments are being used.

As with other ratios, these ratios are based on accounting information and hence rely on the particular accounting criteria used by the company. However, this could be more problematic in the case of fixed assets' accounting valuation because accounting principles often lead the manager to report fixed investments at their historic cost or at cost plus inflation. Depending on the ability of these criteria to reflect economic relevance and/or industry practices, ratios that involve fixed assets might be misleading.

Another set of operating efficiency indicators could be obtained by estimating the growth rate of various lines reported in the income statement. This would allow the manager to get a sense of how each line evolves, and check whether he or she has a story that explains that evolution.

The final set of operating efficiency ratios of interest here include the ratios that assess *margins,* which we introduced earlier.

## Financial Leverage Ratios

The use of debt in the financing of businesses is called leverage. In physics, leverage is something that enhances the performance of a given force. Debt, as a financing tool, has a similar effect on firm performance (and risk).

Imagine you would like to establish a hotdog kiosk in New York City. Imagine also, for simplicity, that the tax authority thinks this would be a great idea, and wishes to help you by declaring your business to be tax free. You have $10,000 available to use as the initial investment and the

**Table 4.1.** Hotdog Kiosk

| | |
|---|---|
| Equity | $10,000 |
| Debt | $ – |
| Assets | $10,000 |
| EBIT | $2,000 |
| Interest Exp. | $ – |

profitability of your business is 20%. Table 4.1 summarizes the initial situation of the company.

Suppose that, after observing the success of your new endeavor, you decide to double its size. By looking at your account balances, however, you realize you do not have sufficient financial resources of your own to use. Therefore, you decide to ask for a $10,000 loan, for which the bank charges a 10% interest rate. If we assume that the business has constant returns to scale (i.e., if you double the investment, the results would double, or in other words, ROA remains at 20%), you will face a scenario like the one pictured in Figure 4.1.

Based on these results (ROE is now 50% higher!), you think you should push the idea further, and keep leveraging your business. To do so,

| | | | | | |
|---|---|---|---|---|---|
| Equity | $ 10,000 | | Equity | $ 10,000 |
| Debt | $   - | | Debt | $ 10,000 |
| Assets | $ 10,000 | | Assets | $ 20,000 |
| EBIT | $  2,000 | | EBIT | $  4,000 |
| Interest Exp. | $   - | | Interest Exp. | $  1,000 |
| NI | $  2,000 | | NI | $  3,000 |
| ROA | 20% | | ROA | 20% |
| ROE | 20% | | ROE | 30% |

**Figure 4.1.** Hotdog kiosk (Cont'd)

you go back to the bank and ask for another $10,000 loan. The bank agrees to do so, but this time it decides to charge a 12% interest rate on all its debt, given the increased financial risk your endeavor is now subject to. At this point, the financial situation of the company will be as listed in Figure 4.2.

Because your ROE continues to increase, you may be tempted to conclude that debt must be a good thing, since every time you use more of it, your return as a shareholder (ROE) increases, that is, that debt increases the power of your own investment! However, as economists like to say, there are *no free lunches*; the increased ROE comes at the cost of increasing the sensitivity of ROE to fluctuations in the firm's operating returns; that is, given that shareholders are residual claimants (their claim is on whatever the business generates after all other claims—employees', suppliers', debt holders', etc.—have been paid), a higher level of debt increases shareholders' risk (i.e., a larger portion of the generated cash flow is committed to other parties).

An increase in a firm's financial leverage will indeed increase its ROE every time its ROA is higher than the cost of debt. The intuition for this is as follows. If an extra dollar invested in the firm generates an operating profit (ROA) higher than its corresponding cost (given by the interest rate on the borrowed funds, $K_d$), the surplus will go to the shareholder, and therefore ROE increases. However, the corresponding ROE is obtained by shareholders, who now face not only the firm's operating risk

| | | | | | | | |
|---|---|---|---|---|---|---|---|
| Equity | $ 10,000 | | Equity | $ 10,000 | | Equity | $ 10,000 |
| Debt | $    - | | Debt | $ 10,000 | | Debt | $ 20,000 |
| Assets | $ 10,000 | | Assets | $ 20,000 | | Assets | $ 30,000 |
| EBIT | $  2,000 | | EBIT | $  4,000 | | EBIT | $  6,000 |
| Interest Exp. | $    - | | Interest Exp. | $  1,000 | | Interest Exp. | $  2,400 |
| NI | $  2,000 | | NI | $  3,000 | | NI | $  3,600 |
| ROA | 20% | | ROA | 20% | | ROA | 20% |
| ROE | 20% | | ROE | 30% | | ROE | 36% |

**Figure 4.2.** Hotdog kiosk (Cont'd)

(fluctuations in cash flow generation capacity) but also financial risk. As a consequence, investors have to be careful when deciding how much debt to use or, in other words, when deciding whether debt effectively creates value to shareholders.[7]

Typical ratios used to help evaluate the firm's financial conditions are:

$$Debt\ Ratio = \frac{Total\ Debt}{Net\ Assets}$$

$$Leverage = \frac{Total\ Debt}{Equity}$$

$$Financial\ Leverage = \frac{Financial\ Debt}{Equity}$$

$$Coverage\ Ratio = \frac{EBIT}{Interest\ Expenses}.$$

The first of these ratios shows how much a firm relies on debt to finance its assets' structure. The second and third ratios indicate how many dollars of debt (financial debt) are used for every dollar of equity financing. The last ratio gives the number of times a firm can pay its interest expenses with its EBIT; this ratio is broadly used by banks or bond holders, since it indicates the confidence one could have that the firm will be able to pay its interest expenses. Analysis of these ratios has to be done in light of the company's overall strategy to be able to give one a sense of a financial policy's adequacy.

## COMPREHENSIVE FINANCIAL ANALYSIS

With these ratios in hand, we can now turn to the question of how to combine them to conduct a comprehensive financial analysis.

Let's think first about a firm's most basic objectives. Since this is a finance book, we abstract here from the firm's mission, vision, or similar issues; rather, we focus attention on the financial perspective. Within this context, we are interested in investors, who put their money in the firm hoping to get appropriate returns, and managers, who seek to deliver these returns.

What is a firm's return? As we have discussed, there are several potential measures of a firm's profitability. If we consider the business as a whole, we might think about RONA, which represents the return on each dollar of *net* assets invested in the firm. What would be the firm's objective with respect to this measure? One objective would certainly be that RONA exceed the corresponding cost of capital. To test for this condition, we need a way of measuring the firm's average financing cost. Given that we estimate net assets by subtracting out all sources of spontaneous financing (e.g., payables, accrued taxes, wages due, etc.), it is easy to see that net investment is financed by two sources, debt and equity. The average financing cost will thus be a weighted average between the corresponding cost of debt, $K_d$, and equity, $K_e$, commonly referred to as WACC (weighted average cost of capital). Summarizing, the firm's first objective will be:

$$RONA > WACC.$$

This condition seems pretty obvious. However, it can help us analyze the way the firm is pursuing its business activity. To see this, let's think about how we can improve profitability. According to this condition, to do better, we should increase the operating result or reduce net assets or WACC. That is, leaving taxes aside for the moment:

$$\frac{\uparrow EBIT}{\downarrow Net\ Assets} > \downarrow WACC.$$

If we formulate this relation in terms of the *areas of management* in which we could work to reach the firm's objectives, we get what is illustrated in Figure 4.3. Thus, to improve profitability, this condition shows that we can work on optimizing the size of the investment (i.e., possibly reducing assets), optimizing operating or commercial efficiency (i.e., possibly reducing net assets and/or increasing profits), or optimizing the financial structure.

One important takeaway from this discussion is that not only the finance division but also the entire company is responsible for contributing to the firm's profitability; it just happens to be measured (and influenced) by the financial division of the firm.

Let's now take a step further and look at the components of RONA. If we take the definition of RONA and multiply and divide by sales, we obtain the following expression (still omitting taxes):

$$RONA = \frac{EBIT}{Net\ Assets} = \underbrace{\frac{EBIT}{Sales}} \times \underbrace{\frac{Sales}{Net\ Assets}}$$

$$RONA = \qquad Margin \times Turnover$$

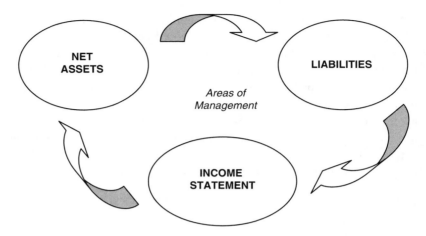

**Figure 4.3.** Areas of Management

That is, each dollar invested in the firm's net assets can generate profit by increasing the firm's *margin* or *turnover*. It is important to understand the lesson behind this decomposition of profitability. Companies generate a return because they generate margin or turnover; thus, trying to improve these is among the main objectives of management. In general, it is not easy to sustain strategies that generate high margin *and* high turnover: unless there are high entry barriers, such a condition would attract new entrants, and the increased competition would end up lowering turnover, margin, or both. On the other hand, low margin–low turnover settings are likely to cause business distress. Hence, profitable businesses typically aim to have (at least) either high turnover or high margin.

While a firm's turnover or margin can be influenced by the company's industry or segment (e.g., supermarkets typically lean more on turnover, while small specialty stores are more inclined toward margin), most of the time the turnover-margin strategy results from individual firms' business policies or management choices. For example, taking the computer industry, IBM tends to lean on high-margin strategies, whereas Dell pursues turnover-generated profits.

What is critical, then, for a firm to ensure profitability? Each dollar of net investment needs to generate adequate profits. Such profits can be achieved either by selling that dollar *many* times (increasing turnover) or by selling it at a good price (increasing margin). Thus, the company can choose to focus on either a margin strategy or a turnover strategy, but it needs to have at least one of these strategies.

To dig more deeply into a firm's performance, we can also look at the components of the firm's ROE. Remember that ROE is equal to:

$$ROE = \frac{Net\ Income}{Equity},$$

which can easily be decomposed as[8]:

$$ROE = ROA + \frac{Debt}{Equity} \times (ROA - K_d).$$

The first term on the right-hand side of this equation is more naturally linked to business profitability—it gives the return the firm generates on each dollar of net assets invested in the firm. This term can be thought of as capturing the firm's *business or operating efficiency*. The second term relates to the profit generated by the leverage choice, that is, to the *financial efficiency* of the firm. How can we think about this term? Each dollar of debt incorporated into net assets obtains ROA and costs $K_d$; that is, it generates the spread between both rates. Shareholders exploit this spread according to the degree of leverage (D / E) selected by the firm. Thus, according to this equation, a firm can improve profitability by operating more efficiently or by making sure its financial strategy adequately supports its business plan.

The analytical framework described previously can be used to evaluate how a firm has been performing over time (i.e., in a time series) or to measure the effect of a specific strategy by comparing the firm's performance against competitors or the rest of the industry (i.e., in a cross section). Let's imagine we are pursuing the first of these two analyses[9]; that is, we are analyzing the firm's evolution over time. The first question we may like to answer is: is the firm (i.e., shareholders) making more, or less, money than in previous periods? To answer this question, we need to calculate the firm's ROE over the last several years. If we find that the ROE is higher than the cost of equity, and it is growing, we might be tempted to be satisfied with the firm's performance. But ROE is not the whole story—it is important to understand the drivers of the business strategy that are leading to the favorable results. If, in contrast, we find that ROE is lower than the cost of equity, or it is decreasing, then we need to make sure we understand the sources of the firm's problems. Thus, regardless of whether the company is generating profits or not, we need to perform a more comprehensive analysis to understand the drivers of, and possible ways to enhance, the firm's performance.

So, what might be a next step in conducting a more comprehensive analysis of a firm's financial condition? Well, one might ask: is the business itself profitable? An answer to that question can be obtained by looking at the firm's ROA.[10] Note that it is usual to see a diverging time-series pattern between a firm's ROA and ROE. There is important information in this divergence, as the difference between these measures is leverage. We turn to this subject in more detail later; for now we concentrate on the evolution of ROA, which will help us understand whether the business itself is profitable (setting aside leverage considerations). We are interested in understanding whether the firm's profitability is based on margin, turnover, or a combination of the two, and how these components evolve over time.

We can start by focusing on the evolution of margin. To do so, it is usually helpful to start by evaluating operating efficiency. We may obtain some relevant conclusions by simply comparing the evolution of gross margin and operating margin. For example, if gross margin is exhibiting the expected progress but operating margin is getting behind (or falling), then we could conclude that there may be problems in the firm's fixed cost structure (or, at least, that there is some *cost* associated with the chosen strategy). That is, the firm may be selling well, at a good margin, but the cost structure is dampening the results. If we see that such a problem is at the gross margin level, we could then investigate the source of the problem by analyzing cost of goods sold, sales prices, and so forth. That is, this analysis helps us determine which details to examine more thoroughly.

With respect to asset turnover, what actually has to turn over are the components included in net operating investment: cash holdings, account receivables, inventory, and/or, as part of the net effect, payables. So, to analyze a firm's potential success or failure in turning assets over, we could look at the operating ratios presented in this chapter, namely, days of cash, days of receivables, days of inventory, and days of payables. In this way, we can uncover where our assets may be gaining weight and we can determine if the extra investment is being productive.

To take an example, say that we find that the firm is increasing its investment in financing to customers (i.e., days of receivables are increasing over time). We need to ask ourselves whether this is a good or bad investment decision. If this investment is fostering more sales (i.e., not delaying turnover), this policy would be fine. If, instead, this investment is not stimulating sales but it is improving the firm's margin (providing financing could be thought of as a way to provide good customer service), this policy might still be judged as good. However, if this additional investment is not increasing sales (turnover) or leading to superior margins, then there is probably something wrong.

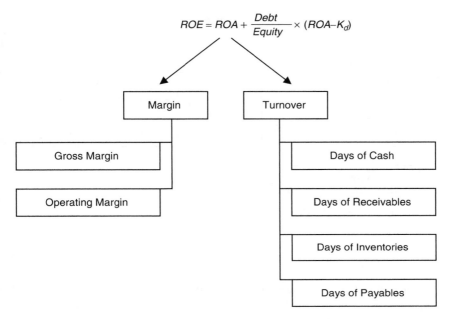

$$ROE = ROA + \frac{Debt}{Equity} \times (ROA - K_d)$$

**Figure 4.4.** Operating Efficiency

Remember, the firm's goal is to obtain a ROA that is larger than the average cost of debt and equity capital (WACC). So, unless additional assets generate returns (either through margin or turnover), the firm is likely going in the wrong direction.

So far, we have learned a good deal about how a firm is operating its business. Figure 4.4 summarizes the analysis up to this point.

To complete our analysis, we could look more deeply at the second component of ROE (i.e., the firm's financial efficiency). To do so, we will need to examine the information reported within the financial ratios category. Since we have already discussed the contribution of debt to a firm's business, Figure 4.5 just summarizes the components of this analysis.

Liquidity considerations come also on the way of this comprehensive analysis. Indeed, by looking at liquidity measures, one can understand how each firm balances its operating and financial efficiency.

With some practice, the analytical framework becomes very easy to understand and implement. When it is used as a standard tool in analyzing periodical results, it can help shed light on why the firm is making profits and how to continue doing so, or why the firm is destroying value and how to correct the situation.

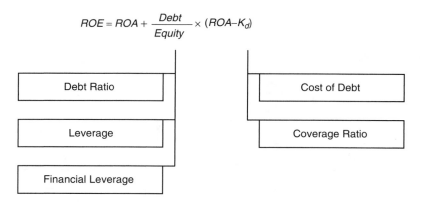

**Figure 4.5.** Financial Efficiency

## FORECASTING

In addition to helping an investor, analyst, or manager understand a firm's past or current performance, ratios can be used to forecast a firm's prospects. For example, ratios can be used by a manager who is considering whether to adopt a new growth strategy, as they can help the manager estimate how much money the firm will need to raise to make the strategy feasible.

In this particular case, rather than use the firm's reports to compute all the relevant ratios, the manager can start by defining the growth target of interest (e.g., a given growth rate for sales), the operating ratios the firm is expected to have (e.g., days of cash, days of receivables, etc.), the expected tax rate, the firm's dividend policy, and so forth. Then, with all this information at hand, the manager can estimate the total required investment (net assets) and compare it to the amount of financing currently available to the business (e.g., debt and equity already invested in the firm). The gap between these two numbers will tell the manager the amount of financing needed to implement the strategy.[11]

Once pro forma balance sheets and income statements have been generated, one can re-run the comprehensive financial analysis to verify the value creation process. This procedure helps firms review objectives such as increasing target growth rates, launching new products, entering new markets, and so forth.

## MARKET DATA

Before concluding, we briefly discuss a few other ratios that, if available, can be useful in conducting a comprehensive financial analysis of the firm. These ratios are based on a source of information that has not been discussed so far: market data.

Market value ratios typically combine one accounting figure as reported in the financial statements with the market value of the share-holders's equity or of the whole firm. Among these ratios are two primary indicators, the *price-to-earnings ratio* (PER) and the *market-to-book ratio* (MTB).

The PER represents how much the market is willing to pay for each dollar of earnings per share the firm is currently generating. If the PER is high (relative to recent history, relative to other firms within the same industry, etc.), we need to determine whether the company is mispriced (i.e., whether the market is overvaluing this stock), or whether there is some information embedded in the price. For example, if profits are expected to grow over time, the market may naturally be willing to pay a higher price for each dollar of profits generated.[12]

The MTB provides similar information. Specifically, when the market assigns a higher market value to each dollar of book value invested in the firm, either the higher price reflects growth expectations or the company is overvalued (which, depending on how efficient the market is, will be quickly corrected through arbitrage). It is often claimed that high MTB indicates that the firm's management quality is perceived to be high.

As we can see, these two ratios can provide insight into the market's perspective on firm performance. Thus, if the firm has available market data (i.e., if it is a public firm), this information will complement the earlier analysis, which is based on the firm's reported numbers.

## CONCLUSION

This chapter presented a method for conducting a comprehensive analysis of a firm's financial performance based on traditional financial ratios. We first introduced the primary ratios related to operating efficiency, financial leverage, liquidity, and profitability. We then showed how these ratios and their components can be used to answer important questions about a firm's past or current performance or about a firm's future prospects. Following this analysis, a manager can evaluate the impact of the firm's overall business and financial strategy on shareholders' profits, or can determine whether a strategy under consideration is likely to add to such profits.

# 5

## Cash Management

Firms hold assets for one main reason: to generate returns. As such, the value of an asset is determined according to its capacity to generate future cash flows. For example, a firm might maintain large account receivables and a varied stock of inventory in an effort to gain greater loyalty from customers and in turn generate more future sales. But, if the main goal is to distribute profits to investors, why do firms choose to hold cash?

Perhaps the first idea that comes to mind is that cash is needed to perform transactions, for example, to pay general expenses and wages or to make purchases. Of course, in some cases a firm may be able to effect these transactions using credit rather than cash, but eventually such obligations need to be paid. Thus, as long as the company *operates,* there is a *transaction motive* for holding cash.

Second, a firm will need to hold some cash to be able to respond to the unexpected. On the one hand, an unexpected event may be bad, for example, if a large customer fails to pay on time. In this case, the firm will be able to pay its bills only if it has sufficient *back-up* money available. This is typically referred to as a *precautionary motive* for holding cash. On the other hand, an unexpected event may be good, say, if a firm faces a profit-increasing investment opportunity. To the extent that pursuing such opportunities requires cash, the firm may choose to hold higher cash balances simply to be able to profit from this *valuable option*. Note that the option motive for holding cash is close to, but richer than, the typical *speculative motive* for holding cash.

Related to the previous concept, a firm may hold cash balances to use as a *hedging tool*. In particular, a firm that generates volatile (i.e., unpredictable) cash flows may choose to hold higher cash balances.[1]

If we consider the development of technologies that facilitate transactions and the evolution of local and global markets that provide a wide variety of hedging alternatives, we would expect corporate cash balances to have decreased over time. However, the observed pattern is just the opposite: cash-to-assets ratios in the United States, for example, have more than doubled over the last 25 years.[2] So why are firms increasing their cash balances? That is, why do firms increasingly find it valuable to hold cash? Some researchers agree that most of this departure is explained by the risk component; that is, it is explained either by this *option value* of cash holding or by the use of cash as a hedging tool.[3]

This chapter summarizes the factors a financial manager needs to take into account respect to the firm's cash management policy. We begin with a brief discussion of the various motives for holding cash. We then summarize the key variables that the literature shows determine a firm's optimal cash balances. Next, we explain why a firm's cash collection policy and its cash conversion cycle matter for good cash management. Finally, we discuss how a firm can optimally invest its idle cash.

## TRANSACTION, PRECAUTIONARY, AND SPECULATIVE MOTIVES FOR HOLDING CASH

As we noted earlier, generating returns is one of the main objectives of a firm. Since returns are computed by taking the ratio between the profits that have been generated and the corresponding investment (e.g., return on assets [ROA] is computed as ROA = operating profits / net assets), the lower the investment is, holding everything else constant, the higher the returns. Therefore, given that cash holdings represent part of the firm's *necessary investment*, it is extremely critical to optimize this balance.[4] Failing at this task would imply either holding assets that are costly to finance and that generate minimal returns—as is typical of highly liquid investments[5]—or holding an insufficient amount of cash, causing shortfalls of critical value. Cash management is about managing this trade-off.

### The Transaction Motive

The most common way of thinking about the transaction motive for holding cash is to use the famous Baumol model.[6] The fundamental idea of this model is that a firm needs cash to run its business. For this purpose, it sets an initial amount of cash, which is used over time while the firm performs sequential transactions. At some point, the cash balance reaches zero or a minimum optimal level, in which case the firm needs to replenish its cash balance and restart the cycle. There are two basic costs associated with this routine. First, the average balance held by the firm should pay its corresponding opportunity cost. Second, every time the firm replenishes its cash balances, it faces some direct trading or administrative costs. The first cost is an increasing function of average cash holdings (i.e., a higher cash balance implies a higher opportunity cost); the second cost is decreasing on average cash holdings (i.e., a higher balance implies less of a need to liquidate assets or run to the bank).

Let's look at an example. Imagine a firm needs $200 a week to pay for its transactions (i.e., weekly inflows fall $200 short of weekly outflows). If the firm chooses to start by setting a cash balance equal to $800, its cash will be exhausted in four weeks. At that time, it will need to replenish its cash account to start all over. Under this setting, the cash balance will move, over a four-week period, from $800 to zero. If one thinks of the payment stream as being smooth, the average cash balance will be $400.

The opportunity cost of holding the average cash balance is a function of the average return the firm can expect to earn by investing its assets, $r$. Thus, the total opportunity cost of holding cash is estimated as:

$$Opportunity\,Cost = \frac{C}{2} \times r,$$

where $C$ is the initial cash balance and $r$ is the return obtainable by noncash investments.

Now imagine that the firm faces trading or administrative costs, $tc$, every time it replenishes its cash balance (either by selling other assets or by borrowing money from a bank). To measure total trading or administrative costs, we need to determine the number of times the firm actually needs to replenish its cash balances over the year. To estimate this number, we simply divide the total amount of cash the firm will be using over the year, $T$, by the amount of cash that is picked up each time, $C$. Trading costs can then be estimated as:

$$Trading\,Cost = \frac{T}{C} \times tc,$$

where $T$ is the total amount needed during the reference period, $C$ is the initial balance at the beginning of each period, and $tc$ is the trading or administrative cost the firm faces each time it replenishes the cash account.

In our example, given that the total amount of cash required by the firm over the year is $10,400 (= $200 per week × 52 weeks), and given that each time the firm picks up cash it obtains $800, we can conclude that the firm will pay trading or administrative costs 13 times a year. If we assume these costs are equal to $100, then total annual administrative costs will amount to $1,300.

Putting everything together, the cash manager should try to choose the level of cash balances, C, that minimizes the following total cost function:

$$Total\ Cost = \frac{C}{2} \times r + \frac{T}{C} \times tc.$$

Figure 5.1 depicts the total cost function and its individual components.

The following formula gives the optimal (cost-minimizing) cash balances:

$$C = \sqrt{\frac{2 \times T \times tc}{r}}.$$

According to this expression, the optimal investment in cash balances depends *positively* on the total amount of cash a firm needs to fulfill its transactions, T, and on the level of trading or administrative costs, tc, and depends *inversely* on the opportunity cost of holding cash, r. Consequently, a firm whose activity requires a high level of cash transactions will require

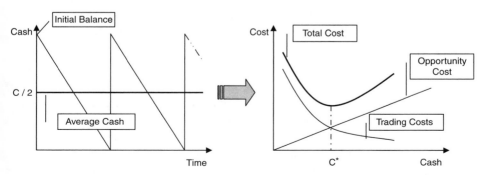

**Figure 5.1.** Baumol Model

superior average cash holdings.[7] The same would hold for a firm operating in an environment in which trading or administrative costs are high. In contrast, the higher the opportunity cost of holding cash is, the lower the cash balance a firm will be willing to hold. Note that it has been widely recognized that there are economies of scale associated with the transaction motive; thus, cash-to-asset ratios should be negatively related to size.

Despite the interesting insights emerging from this model, it has several shortcomings. The main limitation arises from the assumption of disbursements being predictable and performed at a constant rate.[8] Thus, the less this pattern resembles the real cash needs of a particular business, the more we would need to adjust the corresponding conclusions.

### The Precautionary Motive

As we mentioned earlier, firms also hold cash for precautionary reasons, that is, to be able to cover adverse shocks or simple fluctuations around expected cash flows. Intuitively, risky firms can be expected to exhibit higher cash holdings than less risky ones. To analyze this motive for cash holdings in more detail, however, we need to go beyond the deterministic framework of the Baumol model.

The Miller and Orr model builds on Baumol's approach, introducing a stochastic cash flow. In particular, cash inflows and outflows are allowed to fluctuate randomly on a daily basis.[9] Following this model, financial managers are able to determine not only optimal cash balances but also *lower* and *upper* limits between which this balance should be allowed to fluctuate. Thus, this model implies that every time the cash balance reaches one of these limits, the firm should rebalance its level of cash holdings toward the target value. This is represented in Figure 5.2.

Similar to the Baumol model, the Miller and Orr model suggests optimal cash targets that have a positive relation with the level of trading and administrative costs and a negative relation with the forgone interest rate. Additionally, however, this stochastic version of transaction demand suggests a positive relation between optimal cash balances and the variance of daily cash flows.

### The Speculative Motive and the Option Value of Cash

The influence of risk on cash holdings does not come only from the *negative* side; firms can also have *positive* shocks such as favorable investment or growth opportunities. Firms that wish to profit from these opportunities may choose to hold higher cash balances simply because cash gives them the option to invest or produce in "goods states of the world." Some empirical proxies for the level of a firm's growth opportunities are

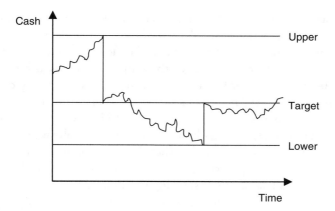

**Figure 5.2.** Miller and Orr Model

the degree of research and development (R&D) investment (normally, R&D activities aim at generating abnormal returns) and the market-to-book ratio (MTB).

Further, given that the option value of cash increases with uncertainty, firms with more volatile cash flows have incentives to hold more cash. Potential measures of uncertainty come from estimation of the standard deviation of cash flow or sales. We expect cash holdings to be positively related to the resulting variable.

Recent studies assign to this option value of cash holding a relevant explanatory role behind increasing cash holding patterns.

### Understanding Cash Holding as a Hedging Tool

In what determines the firm's outcome, numerous variables are not under the firm's control. Many of these variables are subject to random movements that are not easily predictable by the firm; these variables are referred to as *risk factors*.

As we discussed earlier, one way to minimize the negative effect induced by the fluctuations of risk factors is to maintain a sufficient amount of cash to cover an unexpected reduction in the firm's cash flows. That is, one way to reduce the probability of entering financial distress or of being unable to profit from good states of the world and/or investment opportunities is to hold adequate cash reserves, or financial slack.

Let's imagine two firms that focus on oil exploration and exploitation. The lower the price of oil is, all else equal, the lower the expected cash flows. Now let's assume one of the firms holds a considerable reserve of cash (and/or highly liquid financial investments) as a form of insurance in the case of problems, while the other does not. We can presume that the firm holding higher cash balances will be better able to survive unfavorable price movements. But the financial slack has some implicit costs, and thus when oil prices are high, the illiquid firm may exhibit higher returns (since it does not face the opportunity costs of holding cash).[10]

There is, however, an alternative way of benefiting from financial slack. If it is used as a hedging tool, which obtains by setting a conservative capital structure, firms with low or no leverage will have more capacity to raise the necessary funds in either the financial or debt markets. Of course, this has analogous costs, since the firm may be forced to choose nonoptimal financial structures, giving up some value.

To conclude, cash holdings may also play an important role as part of a more comprehensive corporate risk management strategy. This, in turn, is another factor explaining increasing cash holding patterns over time.

## THE PRESENCE OF FINANCIAL FRICTIONS

From the previous discussion, we know that based on the *transactional demand* for cash, firms facing liquidity constraints (the cost of raising funds that are needed to perform today's transactions) should hold more cash. These cash holdings allow the firm to respond to unexpected shocks; in particular, they allow the firm to cover unexpected expenses and they also give the firm the option to produce in good states of the world.

Note that these arguments are distinct from the most common argument linked to financing constraints, which relates more directly to the costs of the funds that the firm needs for tomorrow. According to the *precautionary investment* motive for holding cash, firms facing long-run financial frictions hold cash in order to be able to pursue future investment opportunities. Thus, financing frictions increase firms' optimal cash balances for more than one reason: precautionary investment *and* precautionary transaction motives.[11] A key firm characteristic that influences optimal cash holdings under this view is the extent of the relationships the firm has developed with the financial system. Holding everything else constant, the closer the firm's relations with the financial system are, the lower we can presume financial frictions to be.

## THE KEY VARIABLES THAT DETERMINE OPTIMAL CASH HOLDINGS—A SUMMARY

The previous discussion suggests a number of key relations between firm characteristics and a firm's optimal cash holdings. Summarizing, firms are expected to maintain *higher* cash balances, if:

- they have high levels of cash-based transactions (i.e., cash inputs and/or expenses),
- they are small,
- they have volatile cash flows,
- their MTB ratio is high,
- their R&D investment is high, and
- they have a weak relation with banks and financial investors.

Previous research has also linked higher cash balances to[12]:

- firms with a high cash flow–to–assets ratio,
- firms with low net working capital to assets, since these assets are potential substitutes for cash,
- firms with low leverage if cash is used to cancel debt, and
- firms with high leverage if cash is used as a hedging tool against risks of financial distress.

## THE ROLE OF CASH CONVERSION AND COLLECTION IN CASH MANAGEMENT

A financial manager can assess the firm's cash requirements through cash forecasting. There are three basic ingredients to such forecasts: cash inflows, cash outflows, and the timeline of interest. To generate adequate cash forecasts, the firm needs to estimate future capital expenditures and operating expenses. However, the firm also needs to take into account its cash conversion cycle, which is the length of time between the payment of account payables and the collection of account receivables. To estimate this conversion cycle, the firm needs to determine how long it takes each noncash operating account (i.e., account receivables, inventory, and account payables) to be converted into cash (Figure 5.3). More specifically, the firm needs to know how long it takes for inventory to be transformed into sales, and how long it takes for sales (initially translated into receivables) to be translated into cash inflows. The firm also needs to have a precise idea of when purchases will actually require payment.

Note that to compute suitable inflows and outflows, it is not enough to know the conditions under which the firm generally operates (either when buying or selling products); the manager also needs to understand what is implied by the *cash collection* procedure. Many times, sales that are not done on credit require check collection. If a customer pays with a check, this will need to be sequentially processed within the firm, at the firm's bank, and at the clearing system. The whole process may take a few days before the float (i.e., the money in transit through the banking

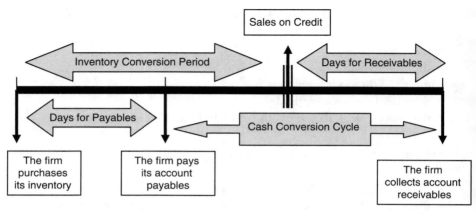

**Figure 5.3.** The Cash Conversion Cycle

system) is actually available to the firm. The financial manager will work toward minimizing its float, or unavailable *collected* funds.[13]

### INVESTING IDLE CASH

Cash requirements that derive from precautionary or speculative motives can usually be satisfied in the form of liquid financial investments, that is, investments that can be easily liquidated into cash. However, given that many businesses experience seasonal cash requirements, which may result from seasonal payments and/or collections that are not matched with each other, cash managers are often concerned about finding efficient ways of storing excess cash (as well as maintaining access to short-term borrowing). Hence, there are situations in which firms find it optimal to invest part of their liquid balances in the form of marketable securities, which provide a certain return and can be converted into cash at very short notice. Since the reasons for these investments are closely connected to the motives for holding liquidity, only those investments that satisfy the attributes of safety and liquidity should be considered.

### The Emerging Market Case and Inflation

Safe and liquid marketable securities are typically readily available in developed economies. Moreover, when a firm invests in marketable securities in these markets, it usually gets protected against inflation (since the return offered by these securities compensates for expected inflation rates). In the context of emerging markets, however, things are usually more complicated. For instance, some local governments are incapable of issuing risk-free securities (default risk is always present); liquidity risk is significantly higher (because of the smaller size and profundity of these markets); and purchasing power is more likely to be eroded (inflation rates are much higher and unpredictable). Indeed, inflation is a big problem for cash managers in emerging economies: under inflation, holding liquid assets not only implies facing opportunity costs but might also entail positive costs in terms of purchasing power.

To get a sense of the degree of inflation risk that a firm faces, one can look at the firm's *quick ratio*. Recall that in the previous chapter, when talking about liquidity indexes, we defined the *quick ratio* as:

$$Quick\ Ratio = \frac{Current\ Assets - Inventory}{Current\ Liabilities}.$$

If we look at the numerator, we observe that, after subtracting inventory, we are left with the most liquid operating assets of the firm. Moreover, we are left with those assets that are more highly exposed to inflationary risk; that is, when the inflation rate increases, these assets are more likely to lose some of their value. Likewise, in the denominator, we have liabilities that are subject to inflation: when inflation goes up, the real value of these financial obligations decreases. Now, imagine the firm has a quick ratio greater than one. In this case, under higher inflation rates the loss in value of the liquid assets is greater than the loss in value of the liquid debts; consequently, the firm is worse off. In contrast, if the quick ratio is less than one, inflation improves the firm's financial condition. Therefore, quick ratios provide an indication of the degree of a firm's inflationary exposure. At some points in time and in some economies, this exposure can affect a firm's cash holding policy.

### CONCLUSION

Cash is increasingly being held by corporations. But cash usually earns the lowest possible return. This raises the question: why would a profit-maximizing firm choose to hold cash? In short, because it works as a necessary *fuel* that helps other assets or processes generate their corresponding expected cash flows.

In this chapter, we showed that firms hold assets for several reasons, including transaction, precautionary, and speculative—option motives. Based on these arguments, several firm characteristics can be associated with higher or lower levels of optimal cash holdings. We also highlighted that because cash has an option value, since it gives the firm facing short-term liquidity or longer run financial frictions the option to produce in good states of the world, firms facing higher levels of risk—more volatile cash flows—may find it optimal to observe higher cash balances. This hedging benefit of holding cash may be particularly critical in the context of emerging markets, where the usual hedging tools are not easily available to all firms. Next, we discussed the relevance of a firm's cash conversion cycle and collection policy for its cash holdings, and how a firm might think about how to invest its idle cash. Here, we highlighted the impact that inflation can have in the context of emerging markets, where liquid assets may be depreciated at a high pace.

# 6

# Managing Account Receivables

Firms usually sell their products on credit, rather than requiring immediate payment. Such a transaction generates a commercial credit (usually short term) for the seller and a commercial debt (usually short term) for the client. The general name given to commercial credit is *trade credit*. Likewise, the commercial credit *provided* is often referred to as *trade receivables*, whereas the commercial credit *received* is often referred to as *trade payables*.

Trade receivables represent a large portion of firm assets worldwide. For instance, using 1986 Compustat data, Mian and Smith (1992) report that trade receivables account for 21% of U.S. corporations' assets. More recently, Molina and Preve (2009a) use a sample from Compustat that covers the 1978–2000 period and find that, on average, the ratio of trade receivables to assets is 18%, which corresponds to 55 days of sales financing. Note that these studies focus on large corporations. Petersen and Rajan (1997), in contrast, use a dataset from the 1987 National Survey of Small Business Finance and report that whereas large firms show a trade receivables–to–sales ratio of about 18.5%, the same figure for small firms is lower, at 7.3%.[1] Thus, according to Petersen and Rajan, small firms provide less commercial credit to their customers than do large firms in the United States, but even small firms provide their customers some credit.

Such a large amount of money invested in providing client financing presents an interesting puzzle. Why would a firm that is not in the business of lending money be interested in extending financing to other firms? Moreover, why would clients be willing to get financing from these nonfinancial institutions, particularly if banks are known to have clear scale and information advantages in lending money? This puzzle has triggered an interesting body of research that seeks to explain the existence and main patterns of commercial, or trade, credit.

In early work on the subject, Meltzer (1960) finds that firms with better access to financial credit redistribute it to less favored firms via commercial credit. More recent work finds evidence consistent with the redistribution explanation of trade credit. However, trade credit may also have other explanations. For instance, the use of trade credit can help firms fight for market share—a firm that seeks to grow at the expense of another firm's business may seek to increase its sales by increasing the financing it offers clients. Similarly, firms facing profitability problems may seek to increase sales or market share by increasing the provision of commercial credit to clients (Petersen and Rajan, 1997; Molina and Preve, 2009a). Molina and Preve (2009a) find evidence that this trend reverses, however, when firms enter financial distress (i.e., face cash flow problems), and that a decrease in client financing causes a significant drop in performance for distressed firms. This result is consistent with firms being able to invest in commercial credit only if they are financially unconstrained (again, somehow consistent with the redistribution explanation of trade credit).

These explanations of trade credit, along with some additional explanations presented in the next section, suggest that trade credit varies across industries, according to industry competitiveness, and over time, according to monetary conditions. For instance, industries with more fierce market competition should exhibit more aggressive use of trade receivables. Similarly, changes in the availability of financing over time influence a firm's ability to invest in clients. The figures in Table 6.1 show that, indeed, trade receivables vary significantly, both across industries and over time.

In particular, for all the firms in the Compustat database over the 1978–2000 period, panel A shows significant variation across industries in the average ratio of trade receivables to total assets. This cross-sectional variation likely follows from the different forces that shape each industry. For the same sample, panel B also shows variation in average investment in trade receivables (relative to total assets) over time. Specifically, investment in trade receivables to total assets has shown a decreasing pattern over time. Further research is needed to identify the specific macroeconomic conditions and industrial dynamics underlying this decrease in the observed ratio.

**Table 6.1.** Trade Receivables by Industry and over Time

| Industry Name* | Trade Receivables over Assets | Year | Trade Receivables over Assets |
|---|---|---|---|
| PANEL A: By Industry | | PANEL B: By Year | |
| Agriculture | 12.06% | 1978 | 20.02% |
| Food Products | 15.64% | 1979 | 20.31% |
| Candy & Soda | 12.46% | 1980 | 19.94% |
| Beer & Liquor | 10.94% | 1981 | 19.43% |
| Tobacco Products | 11.09% | 1982 | 17.66% |
| Recreation | 25.24% | 1983 | 17.92% |
| Printing & Publishing | 18.83% | 1984 | 17.96% |
| Consumer Goods | 22.98% | 1985 | 17.69% |
| Apparel | 25.33% | 1986 | 17.23% |
| Medical Equipment | 20.81% | 1987 | 17.57% |
| Pharmaceutical Products | 12.29% | 1988 | 17.92% |
| Chemicals | 17.71% | 1989 | 17.85% |
| Rubber & Plastic | 20.22% | 1990 | 17.42% |
| Textiles | 22.10% | 1991 | 17.04% |
| Construction Material | 18.71% | 1992 | 17.08% |
| Construction | 22.97% | 1993 | 16.99% |
| Steel Works | 17.30% | 1994 | 17.59% |
| Fabricated Products | 20.68% | 1995 | 17.33% |
| Machinery | 23.79% | 1996 | 17.08% |
| Electrical Equipment | 22.32% | 1997 | 16.82% |
| Autos & Trucks | 20.86% | 1998 | 16.05% |
| Aircraft | 18.15% | 1999 | 15.58% |
| Shipbuilding & Railroad Equipment | 15.75% | 2000 | 15.03% |
| Defense | 22.09% | *Average* | *17.63%* |
| Precious Metals | 3.48% | *Min* | *15.03%* |
| Mines | 9.37% | *Max* | *20.31%* |
| Coal | 9.99% | | |
| Petroleum & Natural Gas | 10.98% | | |
| Utilities | 7.24% | | |
| Communication | 9.55% | | |
| Business Services | 25.40% | | |
| Computers | 24.41% | | |
| Electronic Equipment | 21.51% | | |
| Measurement & Control Equipment | 24.24% | | |
| Business Supplies | 18.94% | | |
| Shipping Container | 15.98% | | |
| Transportation | 14.14% | | |
| Wholesale | 26.72% | | |
| Retail | 10.17% | | |
| Restaurants & Hotels | 3.87% | | |
| Other | 19.00% | | |

*(continued)*

**Table 6.1.** Continued

| Industry Name* | Trade Receivables over Assets | Year | Trade Receivables over Assets |
|---|---|---|---|
| PANEL A: By Industry | | PANEL B: By Year | |
| *Average* | *17.20%* | | |
| *Min* | *3.48%* | | |
| *Max* | *26.72%* | | |

*Fama and French (2007) industry definition.

As the previous discussion suggests, firms exhibiting high trade receivables are making a significant investment in clients. The expected return on this investment is linked to an increase in sales. However, this benefit comes at both an opportunity cost and a cost associated with the risk of recovering the invested capital. That is, in addition to the cost associated with the time value of money, firms that finance their clients are subject to the risk of not being repaid on time or not being repaid in full. This latter risk, usually called credit risk, is a significant by-product of the decision to finance clients through trade receivables. Interestingly, a significant number of commercial firms lack sufficient skills to adequately assess clients' ability to generate the necessary cash flow to repay their debts, and hence some firms show very large exposure to the risk of client default. The study of credit risk has thus grown steadily in recent years, and some of the findings of this work might help us understand, and cope with, credit risk.

In this chapter, we discuss trade receivables and credit risk. We begin by providing a brief review of the main theories of trade credit. Next, we consider the credit risk embedded in firms' investment in trade receivables, and we discuss how to correctly assess and in turn manage the credit risk inherent in offering clients trade credit. Finally, we briefly review how trade credit can be measured.

## THEORIES OF TRADE CREDIT

As we stated earlier, why firms invest in financing clients when their core business is not related to lending money or providing financing is an interesting question. Still more puzzling is why some firms on the verge of distress (i.e., firms with little or no access to financial credit) invest in clients' financing (perhaps offering less financing than during "good times," but still offering financing to less constrained clients). These and similar questions have attracted the attention of several researchers. In the following sections, we summarize some of the theories offered to explain observed patterns in trade credit.

## A Redistribution View of Trade Receivables

In early work on trade credit, Meltzer (1960) finds that monetary contractions are associated with an increase in trade credit. This result suggests that firms with greater access to financing redistribute the available capital by providing increased trade credit to clients facing increased credit constraints in the market. Meltzer also finds that large firms are more likely to have greater access to scarce financial credit, and hence during contractions, large firms play a greater role in the redistribution of financial credit in the form of commercial lending.

Since Meltzer (1960), several papers on the trade credit phenomenon have found consistent evidence. For instance, Lindsay and Sametz (1967) find that not only larger but also more profitable firms extend more credit to their clients during downturns, and Jaffee (1968) finds that smaller client firms rely more on the use of trade credit to finance their operations. In addition, Schwartz (1974) documents that firms with greater access to capital have an incentive to support those clients that have good projects but low access to financing during competitive market conditions, and in more recent work, Love, Preve, and Sarria-Allende (2007) find evidence suggesting that when monetary conditions become tighter (either due to business cycle or crisis effects), less cash-constrained firms tend to alleviate clients' credit problems by extending more generous commercial credit terms.

Despite the evidence on the redistribution explanation of trade credit, however, the large amount of trade receivables among U.S. corporations cannot be explained by this argument alone. Consequently, several research papers have searched for other reasons driving the use of commercial credit. We continue with a summary of the most popular of these theories below.

## Trade Receivables and Information Asymmetries

Another possible explanation of trade credit is based on an information asymmetry argument. According to this argument, suppliers with close customer relationships have an advantage over financial creditors in obtaining information about their customers' creditworthiness, as they are able to observe customers' orders, payments, and so forth. This informational advantage lowers suppliers' credit risk and in turn increases their willingness to finance customers (see Smith, 1987; Mian and Smith, 1992; Biais and Gollier, 1997; Frank and Maksimovic, 2004; Deloof and Jegers,

1996; Emery and Nayar, 1998; Lee and Stowe, 1993; Long, Malitz, and Ravid, 1993; and, more recently, Burkart and Ellingsen, 2003). In a world plagued by large information asymmetries, this argument seems plausible. Thus, it is reasonable to assume that to the extent suppliers are in a better position to lend money to their clients, they do so.

Let's consider a specific case. In the internet boom of the mid- to late 1990s, several "new economy" firms that were financed by equity only started to look for debt financing. This debt was initially provided by the firms' suppliers. In particular, many internet firms requested that their equipment suppliers (typically, large multinational firms) not only provide the equipment and finance the transaction in full but also lend the firm additional funds. The large equipment manufacturers, which were extremely liquid and enjoyed ample access to the capital markets, felt they understood their clients' businesses better than the financial creditors did, and thus in many cases they agreed to provide the extra financing that was requested. That is, during those years, it was quite common to see equipment sales completed with so-called "vendor financing." Note that this vendor financing pattern is consistent with both the redistribution and the informational asymmetry theories of trade credit—the larger and more stable firms with better access to financial markets and better information about this new industry obtained capital and supplied it to their clients as part of the commercial transaction. However, the interesting characteristic of this pattern was that credit was extended for an amount that exceeded the value of the commercial transaction that generated it, maybe reflecting some kind of bet on their clients' future growth.

### Trade Receivables and Business Relationships

Yet other theories of trade credit are based on the argument that, relative to banks, in addition to having better information and the ability to repossess and resell the goods in the case of default on the part of the debtor, suppliers have a higher interest in maintaining long-term relationships with their customers and thus they are more inclined to extend credit to them. The main intuition here is that while a financial creditor can lend to any firm/industry, a commercial firm can only do business with a reduced subset of firms (many times, concentrated within a single industry). Therefore, offering generous commercial credit terms might be a good way for a supplier to increase its business with its natural customers. Cunat (2000) models supplier-customer relationships in the case of tailor-made products with "learning by doing processes" or other sources of sunk costs. He shows that building such relationships generates an economic surplus for the creditor that increases over time.

Along similar lines, Wilner (2000) argues that in order to maintain a product market relationship, trade creditors, which depend on their customers' business, have a higher incentive to grant more credit to financially distressed customers than do financial creditors. Moreover, firms could decide to provide trade credit during times of crisis as a way of capturing the future business of their customers during postcrisis recovery and growth.

### Other Theories of Trade Credit

Other theories of trade credit are based on price discrimination (Brennan, Maksimovic, and Zechner, 1988); arbitrage based on different credit availability and interest rates across firms (Biais and Gollier, 1997; Emery, 1984; Smith, 1987); and transaction costs (Ferris, 1981). In the interest of brevity, we refer the reader interested in these additional stories to the citations mentioned here.

## EMPIRICAL STUDIES ON TRADE RECEIVABLES

Several empirical papers also address trade receivables. Among the first and more cited of these papers is Petersen and Rajan (1997), who provide a comprehensive examination of the determinants of trade credit. Using data from the 1987 National Survey of Small Business Finance, they analyze both trade receivables and trade payables, and test the theories described previously. Consistent with the information advantage explanation of trade credit, they find evidence that better and quicker access to information makes firms more competitive lenders than financial institutions, especially when their clients are credit constrained.

Mian and Smith (1992) seek to provide evidence on how firms can manage the trade credit process. They divide the commercial lending process into five functions, namely, credit risk assessment, credit granting, account receivables financing, credit collection, and credit risk bearing. They show that firms can manage these various functions of trade receivables by (1) establishing a captive finance subsidiary, (2) issuing account receivables–secured debt, (3) using factoring, (4) employing a credit reporting firm, (5) retaining a credit collection agency, and (6) purchasing credit insurance, either internally managing or outsourcing each of these activities.

In a recent study, Molina and Preve (2009a) examine the effect of financial distress on the investment in trade receivables. Their paper's main finding is that firms tend to increase their investment in trade receivables when they start having profitability problems; however, as soon as they enter financial distress (and start having cash flow problems), they show a decrease in client financing. If we assume that firms that are not facing financial problems have an optimal investment policy, then we can infer that firms in financial distress have a suboptimal policy of *underinvesting* in financing clients. Such suboptimal investment policy has a cost, which is among the numerous costs of financial distress.[2]

## EVALUATING AND MANAGING TRADE CREDIT RISK

Financing clients is certainly risky; clients might not be able to repay their debts on time, or they might even default on them. Thus, commercial firms financing clients face some exposure to credit risk.[3] There are two basic ways of dealing with credit risk in a commercial relation. First, a firm can improve its ability to assess the creditworthiness of the client and establish a credit limit based on the client's expected ability to repay its debts. Second, once credit has been extended, firms can reduce their exposure to credit risk using financial tools, for instance, by selling their risk to others that are better equipped to bear it. Notice that both approaches end up reducing the issuer's credit risk exposure; the first does so by improving credit issuance decisions and reducing the probability of bad credits, whereas the second does so by selling the risk to somebody else. Notice further that these approaches are not mutually exclusive. Whether one approach or the other (or both) is preferable is a function of various factors. We explore these factors below as we discuss how a firm might manage its credit risk.

### Assessing Clients' Creditworthiness

Some commercial firms tend to be quite liberal in extending credit to clients, especially when compared to financial institutions that make credit decisions using a standardized procedure. Banks usually have a credit risk department whose main objective is to produce a detailed credit assessment of every client's creditworthiness; they are expert in managing information on clients at a very large scale. In contrast, commercial firms, especially smaller ones, do not always have such ability. Thus, while some commercial firms are very serious about their credit exposure, many perform very little credit analysis before extending credit to clients.

We present here a set of tools that might help a company assess clients' ability to repay their debts on time.

1. *Estimate the client's potential to generate future cash flows.* Repayment comes from a client's future cash flow. Therefore, it is extremely important to understand the industry's fundamentals, the competitive forces that shape it, and the client's firm-specific position within that frame-

work, as each of these elements has the chance to profoundly affect the cash generation potential of the client and in turn the likelihood of the lending firm being paid on time. This type of analysis could be complemented with a Monte Carlo simulation that, by adding volatility to the main variables of the target business, might improve the firm's cash flow estimation. Notice that performing such an analysis is not necessarily what firms are accustomed to doing. However, when managers are challenged on this topic, they often discover that they have an extraordinary ability to accurately forecast the business dynamics and cash flows of their clients. Indeed, such ability is often one of the basic abilities of a good manager.

2. *Analyze the client's financial statements.* By gaining a profound understanding of a client's financial statement, the seller can assess the main strengths and weaknesses of the debtor. Further, by regularly following a client's financial statements, firms can measure their clients' performance over time. This information allows a firm to perform time-series analysis on the firm's own competitiveness. Further, because sellers usually supply goods to more than one firm in the same industry, tracking clients' financial statements allows firms to compare their performance against the performance of other firms in the same industry at the same point in time (i.e., to conduct cross-sectional analysis). The information contained in these time-series and cross-sectional analyses is usually a very important indicator of the firm's financial health, and in some cases can help a firm anticipate a client's default. For some firms, such analyses might seem beyond reach, as they do not have a policy of requiring their clients' financial statements, much less of performing financial analysis on them! However, firms need to make sure they understand their clients' business in a thorough way, not only from a strategic point of view, but also from a financial perspective.

3. *Consider the information generated in the financial markets.* Many firms, especially those located in market-based economies such as the United States, have securities (either stocks or some type of debt) floating in the financial markets. When this is the case, there is a large amount of market-based information that might be helpful in inferring firms' ability to pay. This information can be classified into three main sources: (a) information generated by the firm, usually including financial statements, 10Ks, and other sources of official information, that is regularly distributed to investors; (b) information generated by analysts that cover the firm's performance, ratings agencies such as Standard & Poor's or Moody's, and any other market participant assessing the firm's debt riskiness; and (c) information contained in stock (or bond) prices that, depending on the extent of market efficiency, is assumed to be more or less complete.

4. *Analyze the information contained in the client's track record.* Client firms that have established a long-term relationship with the seller tend to have a long track record on their ability (and willingness) to pay their debts. Sometimes this information is not systematically collected by the seller, so it gets lost or is subject to somebody's memory. However, the firm can clearly benefit from collecting and analyzing all the information contained in every client's track record. For example, knowing why a client delayed some of its debt payments in the past might help predict future delays, especially in cases in which causes of the delays can be anticipated. Sometimes it is not possible to obtain qualitative information on such causes, but quantitative information on key variables can be easily maintained in a database.

5. *Use a default prediction model.* Since the work of Altman (1968), sophisticated managers (or their advisors) have been able to rely on a tool that separates firms into two groups based on information from the past. This framework, usually called multivariate discriminant analysis, can be used to isolate those financial ratios that have the ability to predict bankruptcy in advance. In particular, using this framework, one can split a given sample into a subset of firms with a high probability of default and a subset of firms that are not expected to default. The accuracy of this model is very high (above 90%, for a one-year time horizon), and it has been used with good results in several countries and industries around the world.[4]

6. *Align the incentives within the firm.* Quite often, the incentives of commercial managers are established around sales figures, without mention of credit quality or the speed (or cost) of collection. Redefining the incentives of the firm's executives on a more comprehensive measure might help improve a firm's overall credit risk and consequently the firm's ability to collect its trade receivables.

7. *Establish credit limits.* A combination of the previous analyses is required to estimate the maximum exposure to credit risk that a firm is willing to take. The usual procedure is to establish a credit limit for each client, where the maximum amount of money that the client can owe at any moment in time will be based on the client's creditworthiness. Then, with such limits defined for each account, more general parameters could also be set. Implementing this procedure is quite simple: each client has an established credit limit, and the commercial department can continue to ship goods on credit until the credit limit constraint is met (i.e., so long as the credit limit has not been reached).

Policies based on these types of criteria are very useful, as they allow a firm to install valuable information-sharing and coordination processes between the commercial managers and the financial controller. Each one of these agents, left alone, is likely to pursue different objectives (since the former usually has an incentive to sell with insufficient focus on credit risk, while the latter is likely to be worried about the ability of the firm to collect credits on time, paying less attention to sales). Good coordination between the two is thus likely to be value enhancing for the firm.

## Limiting the Effects of a Client's Default

In the event that a client defaults on its trade credit, several tools can help the creditor mitigate the effects of the default. Some of these tools might be especially useful if the firms do not feel comfortable restricting a client's credit, but do not feel comfortable holding its risk.

1. *Diversify the credit portfolio.* It is usually a good idea to diversify a portfolio. Consistent with this basic finance principle, banks and financial institutions commonly hold a diversified portfolio of credits and bonds so that one risk event does not have a substantial effect on their portfolio. In the case of commercial firms, however, such diversification may not be easy to achieve. For instance, it might be the case that a firm's only target market is very limited and narrowly defined, so that diversification is highly imperfect and a single event might affect the firm's entire portfolio in significant manner. Nonetheless, to the extent that it is possible to diversify a firm's credit risk, it is a good idea to do so.

2. *Increase the liquidation value of the receivables.* In certain situations, financial institutions require the debtor to present some collateral to secure their credit. This is a way to protect the value of the credit in the case of default: if debtors fail to repay their debt, then the creditor can seize the collateral and sell it to recover some of the value lost. This might not be that easy for commercial transactions, however. The transaction cost of a secured debt is usually quite high, and its effectiveness in protecting value has proven to be dubious, at best. Further, because commercial debts are usually accumulated through repeated weekly or even daily transactions, determining the collateral for each debt would imply a level of transaction costs that could turn this issue into a problem without a solution. In some cases, however, this framework could be applied with some success. Consider, for example, the case of a good that is especially large and expensive, for example, a boat, ship, car, or plane. In these cases, the buyer can pledge the goods as collateral and, if the debt is not repaid on time, the seller can regain and resell them, recovering at least some part of the credit receivable.

3. *Receive contingent payments.* Some financial instruments trigger a payoff following a given event; here, this event can be defined as a client's default on a debt. These instruments provide contingent payments

**Table 6.2.** Assessing Clients' Creditworthiness and Mitigating the Effects of Credit Default

| Assessing Clients' Creditworthiness | Mitigating the Effects of Default |
| --- | --- |
| 1. Estimate the client's potential of future generation of cash flows | 1. Diversify the credit portfolio |
| 2. Analyze the client's financial statements | 2. Use techniques to increase the liquidation value of the receivables |
| 3. Analyze the information generated in the financial markets | 3. Receive contingent payments |
| 4. Analyze the information contained in the client's track record | |
| 5. Use some of the available default prediction models | |
| 6. Align the incentives in the firm | |

(payments contingent on the event of default), which are generally packaged in the form of credit derivatives or insurance policies.[5] The market for credit derivatives has exploded in the last few years. Credit derivatives allow a firm to sell the credit risk of some or all of its commercial credit portfolio to a third party. Using these instruments, a firm can enjoy its original credit terms if there is no default, but a third party (the seller of the option) will pay the debtor's debt in the case of default. However, the implementation of credit derivatives is not easy and their effectiveness in the event of a financial crisis (e.g., October 2008) has yet to be proven.

To summarize, by using a combination of the strategies suggested earlier (i.e., by improving the firm's ability to assess clients' creditworthiness and limiting the effects of clients' potential default), firms can increase their ability to offer clients financing without significantly increasing their credit risk. Table 6.2 can help one quickly recall some of the various steps a firm can take to reduce their credit risk by listing the ways a firm can assess clients' creditworthiness and mitigate the effects of clients' default on trade credit.

We conclude this section by emphasizing that every company should seek to understand how to reduce their credit risk: since it is clear that firms will need to finance their clients in order to exist, they would be wise to learn how to do so correctly.

## FINANCING THE FIRM'S INVESTMENT IN TRADE RECEIVABLES

For some firms, trade receivables are a large investment, and as such they need to be adequately financed. In Chapter 3, we considered the financing of current assets in general (i.e., not only a subset of them). In this section, we focus on two mechanisms that allow firms to specifically finance their investment in clients. These mechanisms are (1) factoring and (2) the issuance of collateralized debt (using trade receivables as collateral for issuing short-term debt).

## Factoring

Some firms, especially when they are not able to raise sufficient money to finance their operations, use factoring to access cash and diminish their financial exposure. Essentially, factoring implies that the firm transfers its right to collect its trade receivables to a third party. Implementation of this process varies depending on the local laws, but the basic idea is essentially as follows: after transferring its credit collection rights, the firm notifies the debtor that the credit collector is now another institution. The original creditor (i.e., the seller of the good) collects its credit in advance, at a discount, from the new creditor (the intermediary), who now retains the credit from the debtor (who he or she now finances).

Factoring can be done with or without recourse to the original creditor. The basic difference between these scenarios relates to who bears the credit risk of the transaction. In the case of factoring without recourse, the new creditor takes not only the credit but also the corresponding risk. In the case of factoring with recourse, however, the credit risk remains in the hands of the original creditor; thus, if the debtor defaults, the original creditor (the seller of the good) becomes the debtor of the new creditor (the intermediary). Obviously, the price of the transaction reflects whether the new creditor is taking the risk or not.

Another difference between factoring with or without recourse is the way the factoring is reflected in the balance sheet of the original creditor. If the credit is sold without recourse, the seller of the goods writes off the trade receivables from his or her balance sheet and records the cash received from the factoring company; essentially, this type of transaction is just a sale of the credit to a third party. If the credit is sold with recourse, in contrast, the seller will receive the cash and keep the trade receivables plus the short-term debt until the debtor repays the debt to the new creditor. Only at the time of repayment are both the debt and the credit removed from the balance sheet. In this case, the firm essentially outsources its credit collection and financing, retaining the credit risk.

## Trade Receivables as Collateral for Issuing Short-term Debt

Trade receivables are an asset, and hence they can be used as collateral for issuing short-term debt.[6] This transaction can be packaged in several different ways, but one of the most popular is to set up a *trust*. Using this structure, the seller constitutes a new company or SPV (special purpose vehicle), whose assets are the trade receivables, against which it can issue short-term bonds (i.e., bonds that are guaranteed by those receivables).

Because designing, creating, and administering trusts is a fairly detailed task that is outside the focus of this book, we refer the interested reader to the abundant literature on trusts.

## MEASURING TRADE RECEIVABLES

How do we measure the amount of credit that firms offer their clients? Typically, analysts measure trade credit using *days of trade credit*, which is computed as:

$$Days\ of\ Trade\ Credit = \frac{Trade\ Credit}{Daily\ Sales}.$$

This equation is a function of trade credit and daily sales. Trade credit is fairly easy to obtain, as we can use the figure in the balance sheet at year-end. The level of daily sales is a little trickier. Obviously, we do not observe a firm's daily sales, so we typically rely on proxies for this figure. The usual proxy is computed as:

$$Days\ Sales = \frac{Yearly\ Sales}{360},$$

which assumes that the firm sells 360 days of the year. The trade credit ratio also assumes that all sales are made on credit.[7] Using this measure of days of trade credit, an estimate of, say, 55 days means that the firms take an average of 55 days to collect its credit from clients.

Notice that trade receivables can be measured ex post, as in the equation given previously, or ex ante, such as when we need to estimate the investment in financial needs for operation required for a given project or when we need to prepare next year's budget. The importance of these estimations is usually underestimated. Managers tend to be very precise in estimating the investment required for fixed assets (also called CAPEX, short for capital expenditures), but their precision in estimating the investment required for current assets is usually less precise. To correctly estimate the required level of trade receivables, we only need to have values for two variables: the daily level of sales and the number of days that clients can take (on average) before repaying their bills, that is, the days of trade receivables. Using these two variables, we can recover the expected level of trade receivables at the next fiscal year-end by solving:

$$Trade\ Receivables = Daily\ Sales \times Days\ of\ Trade\ Receivables.$$

Details on trade receivables forecasting are discussed in greater detail in Chapter 4, where we present capital budgeting for current assets.

## CONCLUSION

This chapter discussed the main issues related to the commercial, or trade, credit that firms offer their clients. In particular, we explored some of the reasons for its existence, as suggested by prior theoretical and empirical work on trade credit, and we drew attention to the credit risk embedded in these transactions. We then presented several ways a firm can improve its ability to assess clients' creditworthiness or mitigate the effect of a client's default on its cash flow, and we discussed how firms can finance their investment in trade receivables. Finally, we briefly reviewed how a firm can measure its trade credit.

# 7

## Managing Inventories

### INVENTORY MANAGEMENT TECHNIQUES

A firm's inventory may take different forms. For instance, a manufacturing firm's inventory is likely to consist of raw materials, which are inputs to the production process; work in progress, which are unfinished goods that are in the process of being produced at the time the balance sheets are closed; and finished goods, which are goods that the firm has produced and is ready to ship.[1] Retailers typically have only finished goods in their inventory, as they do not add value through a manufacturing process. And service firms generally have no goods to store. Together with investments in cash holdings and receivables, investment in inventory constitutes the main operating investment of many firms. Why is such an investment so important to a firm? Well, inventory balances can help firms meet variation in demand, as well as variation in the supply of raw materials. They can also allow for flexibility in the production schedule, and they can allow a firm to take advantage of economies related to purchase order size. Yet not all types of inventory are easy to turn into cash. For example, while raw materials that are near-commodities are typically liquid, finished goods may or may not be easy to sell quickly without a considerable discount (e.g., airplanes are less liquid than computers, and computers are less liquid than candies), and works in progress tend to be highly illiquid. Thus, cash invested in inventory holdings may be tied up for a considerable amount of time.

Inventory management involves the setting of inventory levels so as to maximize the benefits while minimizing the costs of holding inventory. Inventory management is important to most firms, for a diverse set of reasons. For example, firms that sell goods associated with high obsolescence rates (e.g., high-technology goods or goods related to fashion trends) need to take care to not set inventory levels so high that they could suffer significant losses in terms of inventory obsolescence. In addition, firms that sell perishable goods need to avoid inventory levels that far exceed short-term demand to avoid losses from perished inventory. On the other hand, firms that sell goods that are hard to access (e.g., because they take a long time to produce, they require imported materials with a long backlog time, etc.) need to manage inventory levels to avoid losing sales. These examples show that while different firms may have different reasons to pursue inventory management, determining optimal inventory levels is quite important for most firms, especially for those whose profits are largely based on asset rotation rather than margin on sales, as in the case of retailers.

So how does a firm go about managing its inventory? There are many techniques for inventory management. Some firms do not set an explicit inventory policy, but instead purchase inputs or goods on an as-needed basis. If inputs or goods can be accessed immediately and goods can be sold at once, this mechanism might work efficiently. The effectiveness of such a system depends on factors such as potential quantity discounts, which would be missed if orders are in small lots, and potential costs of stock-out.

Other firms, in contrast, prefer to buy large quantities to take advantage of size discounts and to avoid stock-out problems. However, this strategy might involve storage and obsolescence costs. Additionally, absent a mechanism to determine the optimal size and composition of inventory, this technique may lead to overinvestment problems, specifically, the cost of financing larger-than-needed investment in inventory.[2]

A third way firms can manage their inventory is to follow the *ABC approach*. To do so, a firm divides its inventory into three classes—A, B, and C—based on annual volume in monetary terms (estimated as annual demand multiplied by unit cost). Class A consists of items that have a large effect on total inventory value, class B consists of items that have less of an effect on inventory value, and class C includes items that contribute little to total inventory value. Based on this classification, firms maintain tighter physical control over the class A items, that is, those items that contribute most to inventory value. Thus, for example, a firm using this approach may forecast the demand for class A items more closely, or may decide to forge closer relationships with the suppliers of these items.

In a fourth approach, many firms manage their inventory by combining the previous technique with cycle counting. Cycle counting involves physically counting a subset of the total stock of inventory at predetermined points in time. This combined approach helps a firm maintain accurate inventory records and identify and resolve inventory stock-outs on a timely basis.

Some firms may manage their inventory using more sophisticated optimization mechanisms based not only on cost-benefit analysis but also on risk-return analysis. To perform such an approach, many inputs are needed, such as supply and demand functions, failure and obsolescence rates, and cost of capital estimates. These inputs can be obtained from specific software applications, or from a customized simulation procedure specifically built by the firm.

Finally, the best-known approach for managing inventory is the *economic order quantity* (EOQ) approach. This mechanism is based on the idea of minimizing the total costs associated with inventory investment. We discuss this model in more detail later in this chapter, after we elaborate on the specific costs of inventory investment.

While detailed recommendations for inventory management are beyond the scope of this book, in this chapter we present some of the factors that have a bearing on the subject. Specifically, in the next section we discuss different ways to measure inventory. We then discuss the main costs of holding inventory and the most common method for managing inventory. Finally, we discuss the use of inventory for hedging purposes and additional considerations related to optimal inventory levels.

## MEASURING INVENTORY

Before a firm can think about optimal investment in inventory, it needs to define a sensible measure of its inventory balances.

Recall from our discussion on operating efficiency ratios in Chapter 4 that firms commonly summarize the firm's inventory using *days of inventory* and *inventory turnover*. The first of these measures, days of inventory, is calculated by dividing the inventory account on the assets side of the balance sheet by the daily cost of goods sold (CGS); that is:

$$Days\ of\ Inventory = \frac{Inventories}{CGS/360}.$$

This figure can be interpreted as the average number of days a firm can continue selling based on the inventory it has in its warehouse, or the average number of days it takes a firm to turn over its inventory. This number varies across firms depending on (1) the characteristics of the good itself (e.g., whether it suffers from quick obsolescence, whether it requires more time to build, etc.), (2) the competitive environment of the industry (which will determine, for example, potential losses from stock-outs), (3) firms' idiosyncratic strategies (consider, for example, the case of Hewlett-Packard versus Dell, commented in Chapter 3), and/or (4) firm size (e.g., to benefit from economies of scale, new small firms may maintain higher levels of inventory relative to their still modest sales than more mature firms will need to maintain).

The second measure from Chapter 4, inventory turnover, is estimated as:

$$Inventory\, Turnover = \frac{Sales}{Inventory}.$$

This figure captures the number of times a company sells its inventory during a given period of time (usually a year, quarter, or month). A low inventory turnover ratio means that each dollar of investment that the firm puts into the warehouse is not efficient in generating sales, due perhaps to market conditions (if it happens to the whole industry) or to a firm-specific business strategy or inefficiency. To see the importance of this ratio, recall that profitability is a function of both margin and turnover. Thus, turnover is especially important for firms that rely on high turnover to generate profits.

Note, however, that since sales are influenced by mark-ups and other considerations, this figure is not typically measured consistently. More specifically, because the numerator (sales) is computed at market prices, whereas the denominator (inventory) is usually valued at cost, this ratio can overestimate the actual figure. A more accurate estimate can be obtained by using CGS instead of sales. Further, since sales (or CGS) is obtained for the entire year, whereas inventory is evaluated at a particular point in time, a more correct estimate can be obtained by using the firm's average inventory over the year, especially for seasonal businesses. This discussion suggests that a more accurate expression for the estimation of a firm's inventory turnover would be:

$$Inventory\, Turnover = \frac{CGS}{Average\ Inventory}.$$

Nevertheless, managers tend to use the sales-to-inventory ratio rather than this alternative expression. In practice, the sales-to-inventory measure can still be useful to identify trends in a firm's inventory over time or to compare how a firm is doing relative to its industry peers.

### An Accounting Perspective

A firm's inventory balance is linked to the firm's purchases, sales, and initial balances of inventory. More formally, a firm's inventory balance can be expressed by:

$$Final\ Inventory = Initial\ Inventory + Purchases - CGS.$$

Firms may choose from various methodologies to value inventory sold and residual inventory, or inventory held as operating assets. Three common approaches are the *first in first out* (FIFO), *last in first out* (LIFO), and *next in first out* (NIFO) approaches. If the firm uses the FIFO approach, the first goods sold will be the first ones used to compute CGS. In an inflationary environment, accounting systems using FIFO will report lower costs of goods sold and higher margins due to the use of old, lower CGS in the cost of sales. For the same reason, this method tends to overestimate the value of residual inventory. The higher inventory valuation associated with this approach can be useful if the firm intends to use inventory as collateral when pursuing financing choices.

If the firm instead uses the LIFO approach, it will estimate CGS assuming that the first goods sold were the last to enter its inventory. This method allows the firm to compute its CGS close to current market costs. If prices show increasing patterns (as they typically do), the firm will report lower margins, which in turn usually lead to a lower tax bill.

Finally, if the firm follows the NIFO approach, CGS is computed using the cost of the next good to be included in the inventory. This approach can be thought of as a more extreme version of the current market pricing approach associated with the LIFO method.

We note that a firm can value its inventory following other methodologies, such as *average costing* (where CGS is based on a combination of all the goods available in inventory) and *standard costing* (where measures are assessed relative to predetermined standards). However, a more rigorous presentation of all possible choices is beyond the scope of this book.[3]

## CARRYING COSTS AND SHORTAGE COSTS

Inventory investment is associated with two chief types of costs: *carrying costs*, which capture the direct costs, including opportunity costs, of holding inventory, and *shortage costs*.

On the carrying cost side, one of the first types of direct cost to come to mind is likely *storage* costs. Holding a stock of inventory implies the use of space dedicated to this purpose. Such space has to be bought or rented. Moreover, this space probably requires some complements such as shelves, boxes, mechanical lifts, and, depending on the product, even cooling or other specific equipment. Other common types of direct cost include *handling* costs (i.e., the costs of tracking inventory) and *security* costs (i.e., the costs of ensuring that the goods are free of other unexpected costs; e.g., insurance costs). *Obsolescence* that causes value losses can also be thought of as a direct cost of holding inventory.

A type of direct cost that is often ignored is the opportunity cost of investment capital. As with any type of investment, investment in inventory represents a *use of funds*. Consequently, inventory faces an opportunity cost, equal to the forgone return on an alternative investment. This opportunity cost is associated with firms' average cost of capital.[4]

Taken together, the total carrying costs for U.S. firms have proven to be quite large, ranging on an annual basis from 20% to 30% of the total value of inventory.[5] Given that inventory represents a significant portion of a firm's assets, this is an important cost. However, if we only consider the implications of carrying costs, we might conclude that a firm's main objective in relation to inventory would be to reduce inventory stocks as much as possible, as the lower the inventory is, the lower the carrying costs. Yet this is not what we observe in reality. Why might this be the case? The answer to this question lies in large part with the other chief type of cost mentioned previously, namely, *shortage costs*, or the costs of not having enough products on hand to operate. Firms may face shortage costs for several reasons. For instance, firms may fail to complete sales and/or satisfy customer orders simply because they run out of stock of the desired good. Additionally, each time firms replenish their warehouses, they face transaction costs (e.g., the time and cost of placing orders). Thus, in contrast to the case of carrying costs, the probability of facing shortage costs decreases as inventory balances increase.

The presence of these two types of costs—carrying costs and shortage costs—implies a trade-off that each firm needs to analyze. The most practical way of solving the resulting problem is to find the combination of these two costs that minimizes their sum. We discuss this method in more detail in the next section.

However, before moving on, it is worth highlighting that a uniform production schedule implies higher inventory carrying costs than a system that matches production to sales. But uniform production typically optimizes the use of productive capacity, including human resources. Thus, if a company moves from a uniform to a seasonal or other type of fluctuating production program, it will need to evaluate the trade-off between the gains in efficiency and the increased carrying costs of inventory.

## ECONOMIC ORDER QUANTITY

The EOQ approach is based on the idea of minimizing the sum of a firm's carrying and shortage costs. As we discussed earlier, carrying costs are increasing in inventory investment, whereas shortage costs are decreasing in this investment. The aim of the EOQ model is simply to find the minimum total cost.

So how does this model work? We begin by looking at expressions for carrying and shortage costs.

Carrying costs can be estimated as the firm's average inventory *times* per-unit carrying costs, *C*, or:

$$Carrying\,Costs = Average\,Inventory \times C.$$

To estimate the firm's average inventory, we need to consider the EOQ's assumptions about inventory management. The EOQ model assumes that inventory is sold off at a constant rate; once exhausted, it is returned to some optimal level, $Q$. The model also assumes instantaneous receipt of ordered material. This selling and restocking process generates a pattern like the one depicted in Figure 7.1.

As can be seen from Figure 7.1, inventory investment goes from $Q$ to 0, yielding an average value of $Q / 2$.

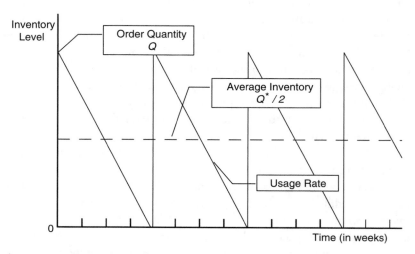

**Figure 7.1.** Selling and Restocking Process

With this average value of inventory, carrying costs can be computed as:

$$Carrying\ Costs = \frac{Q}{2} \times C.$$

Easy! Now, what about shortage costs?

Shortage costs have a more broad definition. However, the EOQ model uses a simplified version of it. In particular, it assumes there are no stock-outs, concentrating almost exclusively on restocking costs. Assuming that restocking costs (including the cost of placing orders and other administrative costs) are fixed at, say, $F$, total restocking costs can be computed as:

$$Shortage\ Costs = F \times Number\ of\ Orders.$$

To perform this calculation, we need to estimate the number of times the firm will have to restock during the year. That is easy to compute. If the firm has an annual demand for inventory material equal to $D$, and if the firm purchases $Q$ each time it places an order, the number of orders during the year will be equal to $D / Q$. Therefore, total shortage costs can be estimated as:

$$Shortage\ Costs = F \times \frac{D}{Q}.$$

Given estimates for both components of inventory costs, we can now estimate the total costs of holding inventory as:

$$Total\ Inventory\ Costs = Carrying\ Costs + Shortage\ Costs$$

$$= \frac{Q}{2} \times C + F \times \frac{D}{Q}.$$

Figure 7.2 summarizes this.

In the previous formula, $Q$ is our decision variable; that is, we need to determine the optimum order quantity, $Q^*$. All the other variables ($C$, $F$, and $D$) are data we need to provide to solve the problem. Using maximum and minimum identification techniques, $Q^*$ can be obtained by solving[6]:

$$Q^* = \sqrt{\frac{2D \times F}{C}}.$$

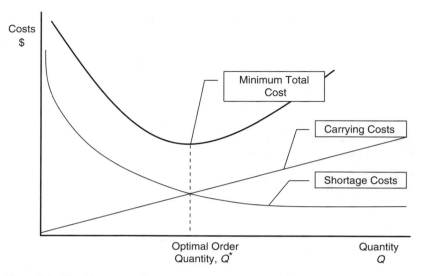

**Figure 7.2.** Total Inventory Costs

Naturally, the optimum order quantity is increasing in total demand, $D$. Additionally, $Q^*$ is increasing in per-order fixed costs, $F$; that is, the higher these costs are, the more the firm will attempt to avoid them by ordering larger quantities each time it places an order. Finally, $Q^*$ is decreasing in $C$, the per-unit carrying costs; thus, the higher these costs are, the lower the investment in inventory the firm will be willing to make.

It is worth noticing that the previous formula suggests some effect of economies of scale: inventory grows according to the square root of its demand, or in other words, optimal inventory grows much less than proportionately with respect to sales. Moreover, the higher the total inventory demand, $D$, is, the lower the corresponding relative increase in inventory (decreasing slope).

Recall that the EOQ model described earlier assumes, among other things, that restocking is performed when inventory is completely exhausted. However, while in reality this might be ideal (it would help in minimizing average holdings), it is usually not the case. Indeed, it is common to find firms placing orders according to some predetermined *lead time*. Taking such behavior into account would naturally alter our previous results, but the basic idea remains the same: the order will be placed not at the time when inventory reaches zero, but at a *given lead time* before the zero boundary is reached. Similarly, the model can be adjusted to allow firms with high potential stock-out costs to set pre-established *safety inventory* levels that trigger new orders when such thresholds are reached.

## INVENTORY AND HEDGING

As discussed earlier, high inventory balances reduce the possibility of incurring shortage costs (though at the expense of facing higher carrying costs). For instance, firms that hold higher levels of inventory face lower risk of having to cease production due to backorders or long lead times. Similarly, firms that have higher levels of inventory have less probability of losing sales due to product shortages. This idea, while not different from what we have discussed previously, builds on the prior discussion by adding a hedging dimension to optimal inventory policy.

Inventory holdings can also help guard against unfavorable changes in the price of raw materials, due, for instance, to changes in commodity prices or to inflation. Indeed, some firms go so far as to decide that, due to the nature of their business, they do not want to hold any raw material price risk and thus they purchase and maintain in their inventory all their product needs for an entire project. This sort of hedging practice is quite common in the case of construction projects, especially if the firm has agreed to deliver the project at a fixed price.

## OPTIMAL INVENTORY LEVELS

Thus far we have discussed many factors that a firm should consider in setting optimal inventory levels. For instance, we have considered how a firm might measure inventory levels, techniques for managing inventory investment, and risks worth considering when evaluating and managing inventory levels. There is no model, however, that can combine all of these elements into a single optimization equation. Thus, as is often the case in the face of complex business and social sciences issues, we simply have several criteria that we can apply and balance in response to changing business situations.

Note that we could add to the aforementioned criteria other factors that may also be relevant to the management of inventory. For example, if a firm produces and sells components for replacement purposes, then it will probably need to hold a much larger inventory than a similar firm that sells the same components to original equipment manufacturers. Consider the case of a firm that sells auto parts for replacement purposes: this firm will probably need to keep in its inventory not only those components used in current models but also those used in still-in-use older cars. Similarly, if a firm produces and sells within a highly seasonal framework, then its optimal inventory will depend on whether it employs seasonal or level production systems. If the firm opts for a uniform production schedule, then it will accumulate a much larger inventory balance over the course of the year, in which case the risks of accumulating such a balance (e.g., the risk of obsolescence, or simply of not selling) will be different from the risks of not doing so (e.g., the risk of running over or under capacity).

Another relevant consideration includes the extent to which a firm can use its inventory holdings as collateral to obtain financing. Given that not all goods are equally usable for this purpose—lenders normally accept as collateral goods that are nonperishable and that are not likely to suffer obsolescence—the types of goods in inventory can influence a firm's inventory policies. We will have more to say on this in Chapter 9, when we turn to short-term sources of funds.

To avoid overstating the case, and having highlighted several examples of the types of factors that can affect optimal inventory management, we leave the reader to think about how these ideas might apply to his or her own particular business.

## CONCLUSION

In this chapter, we started by discussing the importance of efficient inventory management. The first part of the chapter stressed the fact that, like other assets, inventory is an investment and as such needs to be financed by the firm. Next, we presented the main factors affecting firms' inventory policies. Finally, we considered some of the hedging implications of holding inventory, and we provided a summary discussion on various factors relevant to identifying optimal inventory balances.

# 8

## Managing Account Payables

In Chapter 6, we discussed account receivables management. In this chapter, we move to the other side of the balance sheet and discuss the management of account payables. Just as firms sell their products on credit rather than requiring immediate payment, they usually receive some time to pay their bills due to suppliers; the logic is identical—we now just move one step backward in the value chain. Thus, purchases of goods and services generate a commercial credit for both the seller (usually a short-term account receivable) and the buyer (usually a short-term account payable).

Account payables usually represent a large portion of firms' liabilities. In the United States, for example, they account for 9.7% of the total assets of large public corporations.[1] If we also take small and medium companies into account, this figure is likely to be higher, as Petersen and Rajan (1997) and Molina and Preve (2009b) show that the largest firms in the economy tend to use less trade credit than small and medium companies.

In this chapter, we take the buyer's perspective and discuss the costs of trade credit, how trade credit is measured, and differences in the use of trade credit across industries and over time.

### THE COST OF TRADE CREDIT

It is commonly believed that trade credit does not have a financial cost. This is hardly the case, however (indeed, it is not easy to find examples of any source of capital without an associated implicit or explicit financial cost). The trade credit condition typically found in the United States is "2–10 Net 30," which means that the seller will offer a 2% discount if the buyer pays the invoiced amount within a 10-day period; otherwise, the full amount is due in 30 days. This implies that the seller charges a premium of 2% for 20-day credit. Doing the appropriate calculations, this implies in turn that the interest rate embedded in such transactions is above 42% per annum,[2] which makes it more obvious that this form of credit is far from being free or even cheap![3]

This observation raises an interesting question: why would a firm want to use expensive trade credit instead of usually much cheaper financial credit? Put differently, why do firms not turn to the financial credit markets to obtain sufficient cash to take advantage of the commercial discount? Note that this question is similar to the one we raised in Chapter 6 when discussing trade receivables (from the seller's perspective). As in Chapter 6, to address this question we turn to theories of trade credit. Recall that one set of theories of trade credit relies on the information asymmetry that exists between financial and commercial lenders. These theories assume that a commercial partner can have better access to debtors' information than can financial institutions,[4] and thus might be willing to lend funds to buyers in cases where financial creditors leave the market due to difficulties in determining the real situation of the buyer. Taking the perspective of companies looking for financing alternatives, therefore, it might be reasonable to find firms relying at least to some extent on commercial credit.

A second set of theories on trade credit relies on the fact that suppliers can do business with a smaller subset of firms than can financial institutions. Suppliers can only trade with firms that are willing to buy their products, whereas a bank can do business with almost every firm and individual in the economy. Accordingly, in the event of an industry-wide crisis, a bank might choose to restrict credit to the firms in the given industry, while suppliers might be forced to continue trading with, and offering credit to, the firms in that industry, as otherwise they might run out of business partners.[5]

These arguments, together with those related to agency theory and the fact that commercial lenders have an advantage over banks in receiving their products back in the event of nonpayment, suggest that the availability of trade credit is more stable than the availability of financial credit. This availability advantage may explain in part why firms choose to use this relatively more expensive source of credit. Two recent papers— Gianetti, Burkhart and Ellingsen (2008) and Miwa and Ramseyer (2008)—provide an alternative consideration to this question: they provide some evidence that, under certain conditions, trade credit is not necessarily more expensive than bank credit.

This discussion becomes particularly relevant in the case of financial distress. In a recent study that analyzes the effects of financial distress on patterns of trade credit, Molina and Preve (2009b) find that during financial distress, firms tend to increase their use of supplier financing, both in terms of the number of days they take to pay their creditors and in terms of the use of commercial credit as a financing source (i.e., trade credit increases more than financial debt and equity as a source of financing).[6] The paper then asks whether this effect is due to an increase in offers of credit from suppliers or to higher demand for trade credit from distressed clients. The results suggest that, when possible, firms tend to choose financial credit over trade credit. This evidence provides support for the theories of trade credit discussed earlier, as it shows that distressed firms use more trade credit than their nondistressed counterparts simply because suppliers may continue to provide financing when financial creditors have ceased to do so.

The possible existence of trade credit, however, does not make life easy for distressed firms. For instance, consistent with Baxter (1967), who argues that financially distressed firms may find it hard to obtain trade credit, Altman (1984) finds that suppliers may be reluctant to sell products to distressed firms "except under fairly significant restrictions and higher costs, e.g. cash on delivery,"[7] and Andrade and Kaplan (1998) find that one-third of their sample of distressed firms had difficulties with suppliers. Anecdotal evidence in the business press also suggests limits to the availability of trade credit. For instance, a 1997 article in the *Boston Globe* reports that "...the Chapter 11 filing in U.S. Bankruptcy Court in Boston by Waltham-based Molten Metal was triggered when suppliers refused to extend additional credit to the company, which had already slowed payment of its bills."[8] Taken together, this evidence indicates that while firms in financial distress may be able to access credit from suppliers when banks have walked away, they are also likely to experience problems accessing financing from suppliers.

Note the apparent contradiction where, on the one hand, suppliers may help clients by providing credit even after banks have ceased do so, yet on the other hand, suppliers may be the first to push their clients into bankruptcy by not providing credit. This contradiction can be reconciled by considering the fact that financial distress can take several months to resolve. Firms that start observing financial problems typically attempt to restructure and improve their performance; if after some period of time they fail to turn their performance around, they may then enter into bankruptcy. During this process, suppliers are the ones helping firms to continue generating cash flows. However, when they sense that at some point the risk becomes too great to bear, they "pull the plug" and stop financing their clients, which usually forces the clients into bankruptcy. The client-supplier relation is thus a very interesting one, since both need the other to survive but neither can afford to support the other's insolvency.

Being aware of all these issues, buyers tend to be quite strategic in their use of trade credit, and they tend to manage their relationships with suppliers very carefully. In particular, the knowledge that suppliers might provide financing when it is needed most has clear implications for how a firm will set its financing mix during *normal* times. To see this, consider a firm that never requires credit from its suppliers but suddenly makes a request for such financing. There is a strong possibility that this firm will not get the requested credit. The reason is that the credit request might be perceived to be a signal that the firm is having financial problems, which will affect a nonrelated supplier's willingness to offer the financing. Thus, a firm that does not currently need trade credit may nonetheless include it in its financing mix so as to ensure that the option is available at a later date when it may be needed.

### MEASURING TRADE CREDIT AND DIFFERENCES IN THE USE OF TRADE CREDIT

The most sensitive measure of a firm's use of commercial credit can be expressed as follows:

$$Days\ of\ Payables = \frac{Trade\ Payables}{Daily\ Purchases}.$$

However, it is quite usual to see this ratio calculated using daily cost of goods sold (CGS) instead of daily purchases, since CGS is commonly available in financial statements, whereas purchases are not always directly observable and hence require additional calculation.[9] Using this "alternative" specification (i.e., using CGS) introduces a bias whose importance depends on the growth in the level of inventory from one period to another. Notice that if initial and final inventories are the same, then there is no difference between CGS and purchases. Table 8.1 provides summary statistics on days of payables.

Notice how the use of trade credit varies across industries and over time. The variation in trade credit across industries can be explained by several factors. Some variation may be related to different patterns

**Table 8.1.** Summary Statistics on Days of Trade Payables (Calculated on Daily Costs of Goods Sold) Split by Industry and by Year

| Industry Name* | Average Days of Trade Payables | Year | Average Days of Trade Payables |
|---|---|---|---|
| PANEL A: By Industry | | PANEL B: By Year | |
| Agriculture | 47.63 | 1978 | 45.03 |
| Food Products | 32.55 | 1979 | 45.62 |
| Candy & Soda | 39.40 | 1980 | 45.60 |
| Beer & Liquor | 55.74 | 1981 | 48.90 |
| Tobacco Products | 42.04 | 1982 | 46.81 |
| Recreation | 43.97 | 1983 | 51.93 |
| Entertainment | 61.43 | 1984 | 52.31 |
| Printing & Publishing | 51.38 | 1985 | 49.79 |
| Consumer Goods | 47.11 | 1986 | 50.35 |
| Apparel | 34.96 | 1987 | 55.28 |
| Healthcare | 35.12 | 1988 | 53.36 |
| Medical Equipment | 56.98 | 1989 | 55.39 |
| Pharmaceutical Products | 68.71 | 1990 | 54.11 |
| Chemicals | 49.23 | 1991 | 51.77 |
| Rubber & Plastic | 39.60 | 1992 | 52.56 |
| Textiles | 31.29 | 1993 | 55.23 |
| Construction Material | 34.45 | 1994 | 57.90 |
| Construction | 47.71 | 1995 | 58.85 |
| Steel Works | 39.47 | 1996 | 61.38 |
| Fabricated Products | 37.00 | 1997 | 60.92 |
| Machinery | 46.88 | 1998 | 60.48 |
| Electrical Equipment | 42.00 | 1999 | 67.72 |
| Autos & Trucks | 39.13 | 2000 | 69.84 |
| Aircraft | 41.08 | *Average* | 54.40 |
| Shipbuilding & Railroad Equipment | 42.52 | *Min* | 45.03 |
| Defense | 36.88 | *Max* | 69.84 |
| Precious Metals | 67.93 | | |
| Mines | 57.21 | | |
| Coal | 39.68 | | |
| Petroleum & Natural Gas | 148.94 | | |
| Utilities | 48.01 | | |
| Communication | 88.99 | | |
| Personal Services | 38.38 | | |
| Business Services | 75.44 | | |
| Computers | 59.30 | | |
| Electronic Equipment | 54.35 | | |
| Measurement & Control Equipment | 46.73 | | |
| Business Supplies | 40.23 | | |
| Shipping Container | 35.21 | | |

(*continued*)

Table 8.1. Continued

| Industry Name* | Average Days of Trade Payables | Year | Average Days of Trade Payables |
|---|---|---|---|
| | PANEL A: By Industry | | PANEL B: By Year |
| Transportation | 41.35 | | |
| Wholesale | 45.66 | | |
| Retail | 42.97 | | |
| Restaurants & Hotels | 30.97 | | |
| Other | 58.36 | | |
| Average | 49.18 | | |
| Min | 30.97 | | |
| Max | 148.94 | | |

* Fama and French (2007) industry definition.

between suppliers and clients in different industries. For example, if several firms in a given industry have to buy goods from a single supplier (i.e., if there is a unique supplier of a given good), it is likely that the supplier will be able to obtain very convenient payment terms; that is, this industry will exhibit high payables. Other variations across industries may be explained by differences in the goods' characteristics. For instance, things may be substantially different according to whether firms trade commodities or highly customized goods, whether they trade big-ticket versus low-priced goods, and so forth. The variation in trade credit over time can be explained by macroeconomic conditions that influence the liquidity of the market (see our prior discussion on the role of trade credit during downturns) and the incentive of suppliers to finance their clients.

## CONCLUSION

In this chapter, we discussed trade credit from the perspective of the *right side* of the balance sheet; that is, we focused on the financing that suppliers extend to their clients. Supplier financing is a short-term liability for the buyer. We showed that relative to other potential sources of short-term funding (such as bank loans or commercial paper), trade credit is very expensive. The use of this source of financing can be explained by various theories of trade credit.

We wish to emphasize that decisions on the use of credit financing are important for working capital management because they influence the size of a firm's financial needs for operation (FNOs).[10] Indeed, by maximizing the use of trade credit, a firm can reduce its FNOs and minimize the need to finance operating investment with working capital or short-term financial debt. Nonetheless, by paying trade credit off early, a firm can enjoy a nonnegligible financial discount due to the discount offered for early payments. In the event of financial distress, however, firms will be less likely to benefit from this last advantage, as the absence of financing from banks will lead firms to turn to suppliers for required financing.

# 9

## Short-term Debt

As we discussed in Chapter 3, financial needs for operation (FNOs) are typically defined as current assets minus operating liabilities (e.g., financing provided by suppliers, employees, etc.), but they are also equivalent to the sum of short-term debt and working capital. This means that FNOs are financed either with short-term financial debt or with a long-term financing component, namely, working capital.[1] As we discussed, the balance between these two sources of funds is essentially linked to what can be defined as the firm's permanent financial needs. It might helpful to review Figure 9.1 (from Chapter 3, p. 34).

The figure helps illustrate that a firm's regular business requires a stable investment, and thus should be financed, if possible, with long-term sources of funds. In contrast, unsteady business needs (explained by business fluctuations and/or seasonal variation) should be financed with short-term debt.[2]

In the following sections, we analyze alternative sources of short-term financing, as well as useful criteria for managing them.

### SELECTING OPTIMAL DEBT MATURITY

As we have discussed, firms need to make a judgment call on the choice between short- and long-term financing. Criteria that can inform such a decision include:

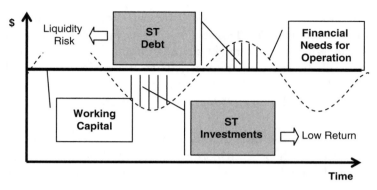

**Figure 9.1.** Short-term Debt and Seasonality

1. *Stability of financial needs.* Long-term capital requirements—related to either capital expenditures or permanent operating needs—should be mostly covered with long-term debt; in contrast, variable needs (arising from seasonality or simple business fluctuations) should be financed with short-term financing.

2. *Level of market development.* The precise point at which the working capital line should be drawn depends, in part, on the liquidity, stability, and deepness of the financial markets. Thus, firms located in emerging or more unstable markets should expect less assistance from the market to finance sudden increases in financing needs than firms in more developed markets.

3. *Extent of information asymmetry.* The choice of debt maturity is affected by the extent of information asymmetry between the *informed* company and the *uninformed* market.[3] Markets often ask for a high interest rate to finance a firm that they do not know very well. In such cases, the firm has an incentive to issue short-term debt (probably at those higher rates) to allow the market to gain confidence in it; then, once the information asymmetry has been resolved, the firm will try to switch to a more convenient maturity schedule. Similarly, firms that expect to be able to release new, positive information (e.g., new revenue disclosure, consolidation of a relationship with an important client or creditor, entrance into new foreign markets, etc.) in the short run are likely to benefit from taking short-term debt until the new information is disclosed. Once the information asymmetry is overcome, these firms will be able to adjust their maturity closer to what they define as their optimal terms.[4]

4. *Market conditions.* Many firms will not want to lock themselves into long-term debt agreements during a high interest rate period. High

overall interest rates can be caused by high inflation or market-wide liquidity problems. Under these conditions, even if a firm prefers to issue long-term debt, it might choose to search for short-term financing until interest rates decrease. Then, when interest rates have declined, managers will modify maturity patterns such that they lock in longer term debt at the lower prevailing interest rates.

It is clear from this discussion that the choice of debt maturity often balances a trade-off between borrowing costs and liquidity: long-term financing alleviates firms' liquidity pressures but is associated with a higher risk premium. However, efforts to balance this trade-off are not always without restrictions. When risk becomes a critical issue (either for a specific firm [e.g., new, small, etc.] or for the market as a whole [e.g., emerging markets]) and the cost burden becomes high, the firm will increasingly choose to use short-term financing (particularly when the supply of long-term money dries up).[5] This implies that differences in firms' financing choices are not necessarily explained by optimization procedures.

This conjecture finds support in a recent study of firms' financial choices across 30 countries.[6] This study reveals that firms located in developed countries have more long-term debt and a longer average maturity than firms in emerging economies. Moreover, the ratio of long-term debt to total financing is higher for large firms than for smaller firms. Given that both small firms and firms located in emerging economies face higher illiquidity risk, their lower debt maturities are better explained by market constraints than by financial choices that aim to balance cost efficiency versus liquidity risk considerations.

Another potential restriction on firms' optimal financing decisions relates to their access to international markets. A recent study on the impact of market liberalization on debt policy, and particularly on debt maturity, shows that on average, debt maturities shorten when economies are opened to international markets. That is, once access to immediate financing is secured, firms are likely to select higher optimal short-term debt ratios. However, the study also finds differences across firms. Specifically, firms with access to international markets extend the maturity structure of their debt, whereas firms that rely only on domestic sources of funds actually shorten their debt maturities.[7] These results are consistent with constrained optimization procedures.

In any case, it is usually easier for a firm to access short-term financing than long-term debt: based on the lower relative risk of short-term loans, lenders are more willing to provide such capital, particularly in a setting of tight capital markets. Therefore, using short-term debt, the firm is more likely to gain prompt access to the necessary funds. Sometimes this is the optimal choice. Other times, this is just the only possibility available to firms under particular market conditions.

We now move on to consider alternative sources of short-term financing.

## SOURCES OF SHORT-TERM DEBT

There are various sources of short-term financing. One way to categorize them is based on liquidity. Some sources of funds involve issuing a security that is traded in secondary markets (liquid), while others include private placements or bank loans, which are not traded in the market. When there is substantial information asymmetry between managers and potential investors, firms mainly use bank financing to fund their short-term financing needs. In contrast, firms with low information asymmetry (i.e., firms located in developed markets with high accounting standards or very large firms) are capable of accessing publicly traded short-term debt.

### Bank Financing

Bank financing represents the most typical source among negotiated short-term financing alternatives. Moreover, the majority of bank financing, especially in less developed financial markets, consists of short-term loans (mainly, and depending on the market, up to 90-day loans). However, since firms commonly ask banks to roll this debt over, it can be considered a structural financing component, but is subject to substantive rollover risk.

#### *Managing Bank Relationships*

To receive bank financing, firms normally contact credit agents and, after sharing all the necessary information (financial statements, projected cash flows, etc.), receive some credit from the bank. To improve access to such financing, firms work to build a good track record with one or more banks; this helps reduce the information asymmetry and build trust between the bank and the firm's management.

More specifically, when a firm asks for its *first* credit, the bank requests a lot of information, including balance sheet and income statements, cash flow projections, investment plans, details about main customers, management capabilities, market competition, demand, and so forth. After collecting this information, the bank analyzes the firm's operating, financial, and profitability ratios (along the lines presented in previous chapters) and prepares its own forecasted cash flow statement to determine whether it should lend money to the firm, and if so, under which terms. Over time, as the firm proves itself to be a good payer, further loan requests are approved through much simpler processes. It can therefore be helpful for firms to start working with a few banks even before they have specific needs for money. That is, given that banks are typically concerned about potential clients' creditworthiness and may be reluctant to lend money before they have a certain level of information on a prospective borrower, a firm can profit from providing the banks an opportunity to learn about it even before the firm has specific financing needs. For example, a firm can commit to send one or two banks information on a regular basis; as a result, the banks would be able to look at the history of detailed information, covering perhaps good times and bad times, and start developing trust in the firm. Then, when the company finally needs a loan, it will have an open path to receive this financing from these banks.

There is a wide variety of different loan agreements. Many firms simply ask for a loan of a specific amount, maturity, and interest rate on an as-needed basis. Some larger firms, however, tend to look for more stable agreements with banks; they negotiate prearranged facilities with one or more banks, according to which these financial institutions agree to extend the firm a given line of credit for a fee. The contract usually specifies the maximum amount of credit, the period for which the credit will be available, relevant provisions (e.g., compensating balance or zero debt balance at certain points in time), and all the other details that are usually included in a loan agreement. The corresponding fees will depend, among other things, on the degree of commitment assumed by the bank. More specifically, these lines of credit can be committed (i.e., the bank assumes a legal commitment to make these funds available to the firm) or uncommitted (i.e., the bank does not assume a legal commitment but simply negotiates agreeable terms in the event the bank provides the firm a loan), and in the first case firms may be charged for the unused portion of the committed funds. The cost typically associated with these lines of credit is based on floating interest rates.[8] Wise financial policies maintain some unused lines of credit outstanding so the firm can address unexpected cash shortages.

## Collateral

In some cases, creditors provide financing based only on a firm's creditworthiness; that is, firms may access financing through *unsecured* loans. In other cases, however, firms obtain financing only by offering collateral. In the latter cases, credit is said to be *secured,* since lenders do not rely only on borrowers' cash flow generation capacity to assure payment; rather, they also request assets to further secure the corresponding credit.

Several types of assets can be pledged as collateral. Typically, short-term financing is backed by current assets, such as account receivables and/or inventory.

Regarding inventory, it is important to notice that not all inventory balances are equally suited to be used as collateral. Perishable goods, for instance, can generally not be used as collateral. Similarly, very specific goods—which have a fairly small and limited market—are usually less usable as collateral. Moreover, inventory is not equally valuable as collateral to all lenders; as we discussed in Chapter 6, suppliers give higher collateral value to the goods they sell than banks do. On the other hand, commodities that are easily deployable and that have a known market value are usually considered to be valuable collateral.

In contrast, when a firm secures a loan by offering receivables as collateral, it can frequently obtain more flexible financing, where the amount the firm can borrow is adjusted according to the amount of receivables that are generated for this purpose. When these balances grow, the firm can make use of more credit. When they shrink (e.g., because some receivables were collected), the firm is forced to pay some of its outstanding debt. One good thing about this type of arrangement is that the available financing increases with the firm's needs, based on the firm's growing commercial activities.

In addition to pledging them as collateral, account receivables can be used to secure financing in two other ways. Specifically, (1) receivables can be *sold* to another party, which is usually referred to as *factoring*, or (2) receivables can be *securitized*. We briefly summarize these two practices in the following sections.[9]

## Factoring

Firms can access short-term financing by selling its commercial credit to someone else, at a discount; this is called factoring. However, there are costs associated with this form of financing (i.e., collection and information costs), which make it somewhat expensive.

Factoring can be done with recourse or without recourse. In the case of factoring with recourse, if a customer fails to pay, the financier (the *purchaser* of the trade receivables) recovers the unpaid funds from the seller of the receivables. In this case, the firm that sold the credit does not unload the credit from its balance sheet: on the assets side, the firm still shows its trade receivables as well as the cash received from the bank; on the liabilities side, the firm includes its short-term debt to the bank. Once the bank is paid by the client, the firm unloads both the trade receivables and the short-term debt from the balance sheet. In contrast, in the case of factoring without recourse, the financier takes the credit risk and the firm simply replaces the trade receivables with the incoming funds in the balance sheet (the cost is reflected as the difference between the amount of cash received and the amount of trade receivables). Naturally, this second form of factoring is associated with much higher discounts than the first form because of the higher risk taken by the financial institution. Usually, only very high-quality receivables qualify for this form of factoring.

### Asset-backed Securities

Issuing asset-backed securities involves structuring securities that are backed by a pool of assets. The difference between this process and the simple collateralization of debt obligations is that, in the latter case, whatever is due has to be paid from the cash flow generated by the firm; only when this is not possible can the holder of collateralized debt seize the corresponding assets in an effort to recover the defaulted credit. In contrast, in the case of securitization, the source of repayment is not the business as a whole, but just the cash flow generated by the securitized assets (account receivables, equipment, etc.); these assets are previously sold to a *special purpose vehicle* (SPV) that is used to set up the financing.[10]

Securitization can be a good way to reduce the firm's cost of financing, especially in the case of non–investment-grade firms: if the risk embedded in the securitized assets is lower than the company's average credit risk, their use will allow the firm to access financing at a more convenient rate. Firms whose assets are mainly short term and do not qualify for mortgages or pledges but have a portfolio of trade receivables are users of this type of financing. A good portfolio of receivables can be either a very high-quality credit portfolio or a highly diversified one (in both cases they constitute good collateral).

### Letter of Credit

There is another way the firm can access short-term financing, namely, by using a letter of credit. This method might be required by suppliers in order to secure their credit. Naturally, suppliers can provide some credit (i.e., trade credit), as we discuss in the previous chapter. However, in some situations, a supplier may not be willing to extend sufficient credit, for example, if customers have not yet proven to be sufficiently creditworthy (there have not been many previous transactions or a customer is simply a new client). In such cases, and assuming the firm has already built a relationship with a bank, the company can ask the bank for a *letter of credit*. This works like a sort of *guarantee* for the supplier, since the bank ensures payment (with recourse to the firm, in case it fails to pay). The usual cost associated with this transaction is lower than the cost of standard credit and depends on the firm's creditworthiness.

This instrument is very common in an international setting, as suppliers typically face significant information asymmetry and this mechanism offers the seller an enforceable payment method: it is probably easier for a given company to analyze a foreign bank's credibility than to assess the reputation of a foreign buyer, and a local bank can be in a better position—than the international suppliers—to assess the debtor creditworthiness.[11]

## Commercial Paper

Firms can also issue short-term *public* debt. That is, they can issue short-term unsecured securities that are quoted in the financial markets. By issuing this type of security, firms can access financing from institutional investors (such as insurance companies or pension funds). However, given that these investors can only buy investment-grade securities,[12] this instrument is typically available only to large firms. Smaller, and maybe less sophisticated, companies could instead issue commercial paper targeting qualified private investors who are willing to take additional risk; however, asymmetric information and market conditions are likely to make this source of financing more expensive. As a result, small firms typically do not rely on this instrument.

Commercial paper typically has a maturity of less than a year. The average maturity is, however, much shorter than one year.

## Bankers' Acceptances

Similar to commercial paper, firms can issue notes, payable either to a specific person or to whoever bears the note, requesting that the bank fulfill the corresponding payment at a specific point in time. Additionally, the issuer can present the note to the bank, asking for its acceptance. If the note gets accepted, the bank commits itself to fulfill the specified payment on behalf of the issuer if the issuer does not pay. Additionally, upon acceptance, the note is transformed into a financial instrument that can be traded in the market.

This instrument is similar to commercial paper, since both are short-term public instruments that can be discounted in the market. However, the risk associated with each one is different: commercial paper is subject to the issuer's credit risk, whereas bankers' acceptances are backed up by the signing bank.

## COVENANTS

Financiers often design special contracts that increase the probability of collecting the corresponding credits. This is normally achieved through covenants, which are agreed upon conditions between the debtor and the bank at the beginning of the contract. There are positive covenants, which compel debtors to take actions that protect lenders' rights, and negative covenants, which limit debtor actions that might hurt lenders' rights.

Most negative covenants are referred to cash disbursements, such as dividend payments, capital expenditures, and so forth. Others are related to the way the firm manages its business. The logic is that, if lenders decide to provide money based on parameters such as cash flow generation, leverage ratios, and the like, it is important that these be sustained and/or used as expected. If the firm instead uses its cash flow to give money back to equity holders (either through unplanned dividends or stock purchases), then the likelihood of banks being repaid might be substantially altered. Similarly, if a firm decides to enter into new projects (facing the corresponding investment requirements), free cash flow estimations will be likely to change and, potentially, so will the firm's capacity to pay back its debt. The idea here is not that the bank wants to *stop* the firm from taking new growth opportunities but that, having taken some risk in the firm, the bank wants to have a say about how the firm manages its cash and future cash needs.[13] Another way of thinking about this issue is that the bank does not necessarily care about maximizing shareholders' wealth; rather, the bank wants to ensure, in the first place, that the firm minimizes its probability of default, and these divergent objectives might lead it to choose different action paths in some circumstances.

Other managerial covenants can be associated with cost management; most frequently, these covenants focus on executive compensation and wage increases. In addition, numerous covenants are related to the firm's ability to take on more debt. Sometimes the firm can overcome these restrictions through a good business plan and/or by properly arranging debt seniority.

In general, managers face a trade-off between the need to access financing (which may lead to some of these concessions to the lender) and the need to allow the business to grow. This trade-off, in more general terms, can be thought of as between maximizing shareholder wealth and minimizing the probability of default, as we point to earlier.

## OPTIMAL NUMBER OF CREDITORS

Previous models have suggested that a firm balances two main objectives in determining the optimal number of creditors it should borrow from, namely, (1) discouraging the firm from defaulting on its debts and (2) limiting the value loss in the case of liquidation.[14] Certainly, a firm's debt structures affect not only what creditors can get upon liquidation of the firm's assets but also managers' incentives to avoid default. If managers are supposed to pay more to stop creditors from liquidating assets when there are many creditors rather than just a few (i.e., if a default scenario is more costly), then having a larger number of creditors may reduce managers' incentives to make decisions that increase the probability of default. However, a larger number of creditors would typically lead to a greater loss in value in the event of default. This trade-off may explain some cross-sectional variation among firm financing choices. More specifically, Bolton and Scharfstein (1996) suggest that firms of lower credit quality should focus more on maximizing liquidation value, which is achieved by choosing to borrow, if possible, from just one creditor. In contrast, firms of high credit quality should concentrate on selecting a sufficient number of creditors that discourages default. Additionally, the authors show that firms with highly complementary assets (i.e., assets that are worth more together than in isolation) should optimally select a lower number of creditors.[15]

## SENIOR AND SUBORDINATED DEBT

When firms search for financing, they can have several commitments at any given point in time; that is, firms frequently have numerous sources of outstanding debt. When this is the case, the various debt series are arranged into a sort of pecking order, which specifies the priority or *seniority* associated with each of their debtors' claims.

*Seniority* is a relative term. One security is *senior* to another when it gives the possessor priority rights to the firm's cash flows or assets. That is, security A is senior to security B if the holders of security A are to be paid before the holders of security B. Moreover, if security A is senior to security B, the investors of the latter are paid only after everything owed to the investors of A have been paid at each point in time. In these cases, we can also say that security B is *junior* to A. The priority of debt series is usually important in the cases of firms in financial distress that need additional financing. The financing obtained in Chapter 11, called debtor in possession (DIP) financing, is usually senior to every other debt issued by the firm and plagued with covenants. This is the only way in which financially distressed firms can obtain genuine new cash to keep operating.

## CONCLUSION

This chapter discussed short-term sources of funds and identified the key drivers behind the most common financing options.

Firms cover most of their short-term seasonal financial needs using loans obtained from the banking system. One reason for using loans is that it is easy to adjust the firm's debt maturity mix toward optimal maturities. Another important reason for using short-term loans is that many alternatives are not available for the firm or are only available at high cost. Small or medium-sized firms, for instance, especially those in nondeveloped markets, cannot issue commercial paper given the information asymmetry and poor investor protection environment under which they operate, or simply because of their small scale.

We emphasized that short-term debt has a strategic role in many businesses; that is, there is an ample set of conditions under which it is efficient for firms to look for short-term sources of funds. However, short-term debt has been considered to be responsible for leading many firms into financial trouble—this is frequently argued not only at the firm level but also at the country level. Yet some studies find that the direction of causality (i.e., the link between short-term debt and financial trouble) might be quite the opposite.[16] In fact, it is likely that firms characterized by lower accounting standards and credit quality suffer from inferior long-term debt capacity. As a result, these firms usually rely heavily on short-term financing, even when they should have issued long-term financing. This suboptimal financing pattern (explained by the mismatch between the maturity of assets and liabilities, and not by the mere use of short-term financing) causes firms to face liquidity problems, which, in many occasions, precipitate financial trouble.

# 10

## Working Capital and Corporate Strategy

As you probably have realized by now, working capital management and corporate strategy are closely related: firms with sound working capital policies are in a better position to finance their operating investment, predate on their competitors, and improve their competitive position. This is especially true in the case of firms operating in economies with inefficient capital markets. This chapter provides an integrated view of working capital management policies and how they can be used to help improve firms' competitive position. Working capital management plays an important role in both the strategic planning stage and the execution of a firm's strategy.

We start by discussing the role of working capital management during the strategic planning and execution stages. We then explain how the working capital management framework can be used to help managers make operating decisions such as how much to invest in clients or products. Finally, we turn the discussion to the analysis of the role of working capital policies as a strategic weapon.

### STRATEGIC PLANNING

Executives spend a great deal of time designing and planning their corporate and competitive strategies. Indeed, it is common to see long off-site top management meetings in which strategic plans are laid down in great detail.

Unfortunately, these plans typically focus on operational matters, leaving aside questions related to their financial consequences. Moreover, many of these meetings conclude without a formal financial plan of the firm under the proposed scenarios. Even in those cases in which some financial planning is performed, it is usual to see the forecasts stop at the operational level, that is, with a profit and loss estimate of earnings before interest and tax (EBIT), as it is usually argued that EBIT captures the operational performance of the firm. However, unless we consider the financial implications of a firm's operational plans (i.e., unless we forecast the corresponding balance sheet so that we can build estimates of the financial needs for operations and their corresponding costs), we cannot know whether a given strategic plan is financially feasible. It is not surprising, therefore, that this lack of balance sheet forecasting so often observed causes many firms to find themselves in a difficult financial situation.

To see how a firm's operational strategy can influence its financial standing, consider a firm pursuing an aggressive growth strategy, as we often observe. The targets associated with such a strategy usually cannot be met without the firm taking steps designed to convince competitors' customers to switch suppliers. In particular, the firm will typically need to lower prices, offer extra days of financing, or promise a more aggressive schedule of deliveries. When customers are allowed to repay their bills over a longer horizon, the clients' accounts will grow; similarly, when firms agree to deliver goods under a more aggressive schedule (e.g., daily instead of weekly), the inventory balance will grow. In either case, the firm's growth strategy will cause the firm's financial needs for operation (FNOs) to increase.

We can decompose the impact of growth into two components: an *extra days* component and a *sales growth* component. To illustrate the benefit of such decomposition, consider the case of a large distributor of candies and chocolates in Latin America, called Razzani and Vera SA (RAVESA).[1] Initially, its market was highly fragmented and growing at a very slow pace. Several years ago, under new management, the company planned an aggressive growth schedule based mainly on capturing new clients in the same area they were already serving. The operational plan was quite accurate, and after two years the firm achieved most of its forecasted operational targets—in particular, the firm increased sales by 14% (from $48,267m to $55,154m) in two years in a stalled market. Additionally, during the same period, the firm's contribution margin and EBIT margin (to sales) increased, implying that the observed growth was not achieved at the expense of heavy discounts, additional logistical costs, or higher selling, general, and administrative (SG&A) costs. The ex post consequences of this plan, however, were quite disastrous for the firm. It turns out that in order to achieve the plan's goals, the firm allowed clients to take extra days to repay their bills. Before pursuing this plan, the company collected its trade receivables in an average of 16.2 days; in contrast, after this period, clients were repaying their bills in 21.6 days, for a 5.4-day difference. In financial terms, the initial financial statements indicated that the company was financing clients for $2,167.0m, while after executing this plan, this same figure was $3,303.1m, implying a $1,136.1m investment in clients. Given that the company did not forecast balance sheets at the planning stage of this aggressive strategy, it was not able to anticipate this consequence of its growth strategy. The company had planned for some operational financing needs, but the calculation fell short by several hundred thousand dollars.

To avoid falling into this trap, it is useful to consider how the company is going to convince prospective clients to switch suppliers in the early planning stages. If the market is not growing and the firm is not planning to offer price discounts, then some sort of investment in client financing will likely be required. Forecasting a balance sheet pushes management to ask the right questions at the planning stage and minimizes the chance that issues such as these are overlooked.

So, how can we build these forecasts? As we mentioned earlier, investment in trade receivables can be forecasted in more detail by separating its *days of credit* effect and its *sales growth* effect. Continuing our example, had the company increased its sales to $55,154m with no change to the level of days of credit (16.2 days), the investment in trade receivables by the end of the process would have been $2,481.2m,[2] for a $314.9m increase over the previous investment, as opposed to the $1,136.1m investment made by RAVESA (which results from the combined "sales growth–extra days" effect). Therefore, the decomposition of the total increased investment in trade receivables can be expressed as:

$$\$314.9m\ (\Delta\ sales\ effect) + \$821.2m\ (\Delta\ days\ of\ credit\ effect) = \$1,136.1m.$$

The same thing happens when we consider investment in inventory. One of the ways a company can convince a potential client to switch suppliers is to promise a more aggressive schedule of deliveries. Imagine that a firm receives goods from its suppliers on a weekly basis. An attractive proposal would be to promise to deliver the goods on a daily basis. Obviously, this reduces the client's need to hold goods in inventory, since it now receives goods every day. But notice that the goods that are not in the client's inventory are now in the supplier's inventory: a larger investment in inventory is needed to fulfill the client's more frequent need for goods. This additional investment in inventory can, again, be decomposed into *days* and *sales growth* effects.

These examples highlight how the days and sales growth effects of both trade receivables and inventory need to be considered at the planning stage of the corporate strategy. Of course, it is impossible to consider the full financial implications of any plan without estimating the firm's full pro forma balance sheets. That is, only a complete analysis of the financial implications of a corporate strategy can allow a firm to adequately forecast the financial effects of its plans. Anything short of a complete financial plan will increase the chance that a firm enters into an ex ante successful plan that, even if the firm is successful in its implementation, will take the company to financial failure because the forecast was incomplete.

Can we make any general statements about how demanding a sales growth strategy will be in terms of FNOs? Yes, we can! This sensitivity depends on the firm's operating ratios. For example, some big retailers, such as supermarkets, typically obtain generous financing from their suppliers; therefore, these firms may even have negative FNOs. In cases like this, firms are allowed to pursue high-growth strategies, since these firms can be mostly self-financed. In contrast, businesses that are usually required to sustain their channel (e.g., *big-ticket*-item producers that need to finance their dealers) find growth strategies to be very demanding in terms of operating investment needs.

In sum, even if days of receivables or days of inventory are not expected to increase, an adequate forecast of the operational consequences of the projected sales growth has to be performed to make sure the firm has a complete and accurate estimate of the funds needed to finance the proposed growth plan.

A few additional implications follow from this discussion. Notice that growth due to increased volume and growth due to increased prices have different impacts on the level of FNOs that are needed. More specifically, increasing prices will generate an increase in the financing to clients since the firm is now financing something that is more valuable; that is, every item that the firm has financed is more valuable than before the price increase. Inventory, on the other hand, does not change since goods held in inventory are valued at the cost of goods sold (which we assume has not changed with the price increase).[3] In contrast, in cases in which a firm grows by increasing volume, both trade receivables and inventory are affected by such growth, given that a change in the flow of goods affects both measures.

## Financing the Expected Financial Needs for Operation

Once a firm has projected the financial implications of the proposed corporate strategy, it is imperative that top management makes a decision regarding the level of working capital that it will commit in order to finance the forecasted level of growth and its related investment in operational assets. Remember that working capital is the long-term financing (either long-term debt or equity) used to finance FNOs. The usual objective of matching asset and liability maturities implies that if the firm is forecasting a permanent increase in FNOs (as opposed to a seasonal or occasional increase), then it will need to find a way to increase its working capital. Bear in mind that one can increase working capital by raising long-term debt or equity or by divesting itself of fixed assets.[4]

If we consider the case of some emerging economies and/or of some specific economic events, it may be difficult for a firm to issue long-term debt or equity even to finance profitable projects or growth strategies, given the absence of efficient capital markets. In these cases, increasing working capital might be substantially more complicated, or even impossible. Such difficulties, however, need to be considered at the corporate strategy planning stage; otherwise, the firm might run into serious financial problems from increases in FNOs that cannot be adequately financed.

At this stage, it is important to remember that whereas FNOs are frequently beyond the reach of managerial decisions, working capital is assumed to be chosen by management. In other words, the theory indicates that a firm should measure the FNOs implied under the proposed corporate strategy, and then choose the appropriate level of working capital. Unfortunately, this sequence of decisions is not always feasible, since in some illiquid and inefficient financial markets it is not always possible to establish a chosen level of working capital. That is, while the strategy should determine the size and riskiness of assets, which should in turn influence the size and type of optimal financing, markets or financial constraints might induce decisions to be made in the opposite direction.

We discuss these issues and their main implications in the following two sections.

## IMPLEMENTATION

Working capital management has several important implications for the implementation of a company's strategic plan. First, while FNOs depend in large part on the firm's activity level and the terms of trade agreed upon by the firm and its trade partners (suppliers and clients), these are not generally under the firm's perfect control and hence it is difficult to anticipate FNOs exactly. For example, actions designed to help the company meet its sales objectives may lead the firm, upon implementation, to experience above- or below-target levels of sales growth. Similarly, unanticipated market dynamics may lead to unexpected levels of sales growth. Since firms are not able to fully control their level of sales growth, they cannot perfectly forecast the exact level of FNOs that will be required. Turning to the terms of trade, which profoundly affect net operating investment, it is quite usual to observe firms assuming stable trading conditions (i.e., expecting the terms of trade this year to be the same as those prevalent in previous years). Yet trading conditions vary significantly over time in response to changes in market dynamics. Because such changes are outside a firm's control, they further complicate the firm's ability to forecast FNOs.

Business experience should help managers better forecast changes in market dynamics and their effects on firms' operating ratios. However, because such changes are largely due to the competitive situation of the industry, a good way to analyze this situation is to use the framework of Porter's five forces, depicted in Figure 10.1.

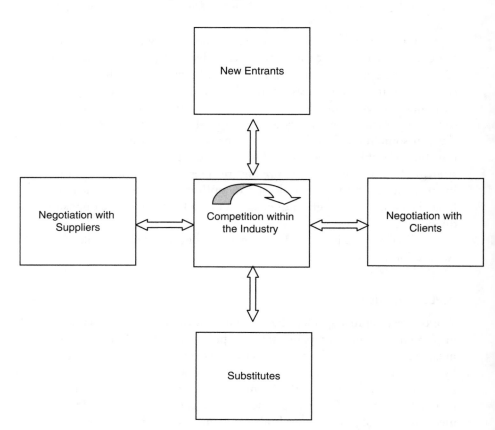

**Figure 10.1.** Five Forces Affecting an Industry

Figure 10.1 shows Porter's (1980) analysis of the five forces that shape an industry's competitive situation. As we can see from the figure, an industry is affected by the extent of competition among its players, the competitive threat posed by potential new entrants to the industry, the existence of actual or potential substitute products, and firms' ability to negotiate with suppliers and clients. Of these five forces, the ability to negotiate with suppliers and clients, which depends on a firm's relative strength within the value chain, is the competitive force that has the greatest effect on the trade conditions of an industry. This negotiation capacity, which is affected by all of the other forces that affect the industry, can be forecasted if management has a good understanding of the competitive market dynamics of the corresponding industry. This implies that even though FNOs are largely out of a firm's complete control, it is not necessarily the case that they cannot be forecasted. The firm can forecast the level of FNOs, and decide the corresponding level of working capital, by choosing the level of long-term capital in excess of fixed assets (i.e., the level of long-term capital financing current assets).

In addition to market dynamics affecting a company's operations, many managerial decisions also have a potential impact on them. The sales manager increasing sales or changing the firm's commercial credit terms, the purchasing manager setting the level of purchases or changing the number of days taken to repay suppliers, and the production manager choosing a different production schedule are all examples of operating decisions that have an effect on the level of the firm's FNOs. The main problem with this is that managers are often not aware of the financial implications of their operating decisions. This is because they do not realize that *every* operating decision has an effect on the firm's operating investment. The only way to solve this problem is to give managers adequate training on the financial implications of their operational decisions, that is, training on working capital management.

Another potential problem that can arise when managerial decisions that increase FNOs are made is that they are simply not communicated to the financial department, resulting in unexpected cash shortages; the resulting shortages can be particularly severe in the case of small firms. Some companies try to mitigate this problem by raising the topic during weekly manager meetings. Other companies require that certain transactions receive approval from the financial department to help reduce such issues.

Implementation of a firm's strategic plan should start with managers forming the operational plan; in doing so, the managers should assess the plan's main implications and identify the tools to be used to achieve the plan's targets. Next, given this input, the financial department needs to forecast the firm's financial position by projecting all relevant financial statements (profit and loss, balance sheet, and cash flow), making sure that the FNOs are adequately considered. Finally, with this information, and a recommendation from the finance department, the board should decide the level of working capital that will accommodate the firm's strategic plan.

Note that this process is based on expected figures. Usually, volatility is not considered at this stage. However, good practice suggests that the effects of volatility be considered in these projections. The more common procedures for doing so include scenario analysis, Monte Carlo simulations, and stress testing at the planning stages. These methodologies can help managers analyze the effects of volatility in some of the variables considered and evaluate potential alternative plans that can help the firm solve problems that may arise as it moves forward.

Finally, during the implementation stage, it is critical to establish specific controls on the execution of the plan. To do so, firms typically design ratios and control panels that help managers identify any deviations with respect to the planned scenario. It is usually helpful to link this control panel to a comprehensive financial analysis, such as that discussed in Chapter 4 (where we focused on analyzing profitability and its composition and evolution over time). By checking the evolution of a firm's margin and turnover, managers are able to assess how well the plan is being executed and are able to forecast corrections in case they are needed.

## USING WORKING CAPITAL TO MAKE OPERATING DECISIONS

By now, it should be clear that FNOs are the operating investments needed to be in a certain business (with a given strategy). When we want to analyze profitability, we typically measure the generated cash flows and compare them with the necessary investment, where the latter should include investment not only in fixed assets but also in FNOs. Yet, when managers make operating decisions, they rarely follow this logic. Instead, we often see operating decisions made without regard to their effect on the firm's operating investments. More specifically, many decisions are based on margins, without consideration for their impact on operating investment. We present an example in this section.

Consider a firm that is analyzing the relative profitability of its different customers (which could be easily extended to an analysis of different products, different geographical markets, etc.). The usual approach would be to estimate the contribution margin of each customer and to invest in those generating the highest margin. However, there is an advantage to going one step beyond this framework. In particular, by estimating not only the contribution margin of each customer but also the corresponding

**Table 10.1.** Per-client Financial Needs for Operation Analysis

| | Cost | 10 | | | | | | | |
|---|---|---|---|---|---|---|---|---|---|
| | Price | Units | Sales | CGS | CM | Rec | Inv | Pay | FNOs |
| ABC | 15,00 | 1.000 | 15.000 | 10.000 | 5.000 | 60 | 60 | 30 | 3.333,33 |
| MSN | 13,50 | 2.000 | 27.000 | 20.000 | 7.000 | 45 | 35 | 30 | 3.652,78 |
| XYZ | 12,00 | 4.000 | 48.000 | 40.000 | 8.000 | 10 | 15 | 30 | 333,33 |

investment in FNOs, the firm will be able to reach a better conclusion. To see this, consider the information summarized in Table 10.1.

Table 10.1 presents an extremely simplified case of a firm that sells the same product (or the same average product mix) to three clients. The cost of the goods is $10 per unit, but the firm obtains different net prices and different payment terms from different clients. ABC Corp., for example, pays a higher price but has longer payment terms than the other two clients, whereas XYZ Corp. pays the lowest price, pays faster, and requires lower levels of inventory.[5] Assume that suppliers' terms do not change across customers (this is a very innocuous assumption that can be easily relaxed). Combining these data, we can calculate the contribution margin of each client. In addition, Table 10.1 presents the investment each client requires in order to achieve that margin. For example, client XYZ, who has the lowest margin per unit ($12 – $10 = $2), requires a negative investment in FNOs.[6] With the complete set of information obtained from this framework, we are able to analyze operating decisions with the same rigor that we use to analyze other financial decisions that typically have a much lower impact on the overall performance of a given firm.

This framework is used by Naturis srl, an Italian dehydrated food company, to decide how to allocate its scarce commercial resources across clients. The company does this analysis both ex ante when the yearly budget is made and ex post (on a quarterly basis) using real figures per client, with very good results.

## WORKING CAPITAL AS A STRATEGIC WEAPON

In economies where access to financing (especially long-term debt and equity) is likely to be limited, working capital management becomes more important than in countries with efficient capital markets. When long-term capital is not available, firms might revise their capital expenditure plans to reflect the lack of financing opportunities, but even in this case they may need to raise capital to finance their investment in current assets. Unfortunately, given the estimation and implementation difficulties mentioned earlier, the increase in FNOs might drag an undercapitalized firm into financial distress.

To illustrate, consider the case of two competing firms. Firm A has FNOs of $100 and working capital of $70 (the balance is covered by short-term financing). Its competitor, Firm B, also has FNOs of $100 but has working capital of $30 (Firm B's short-term financing is therefore equal to $70). Assume that both firms' credit limit on short-term debt is $70. According to this set-up, Firm A has some financial slack (of $40), whereas Firm B is already using all of its available short-term debt to finance FNOs. Now, consider what happens when a positive shock to the industry causes both firms to observe a 20% increase in sales, and in turn a 20% increase in FNOs. Firm A will be able to take on additional short-term debt and serve the market. Firm B, on the other hand, is already at its credit limit for short-term debt and thus, unless it can negotiate a larger credit limit, it will eventually enter financial distress and lose market share to Firm A. Thus, given an inefficient market where long-term capital is not readily available, the more aggressive working capital management approach of Firm B is likely to cause the firm trouble if it needs to finance growing FNOs. This easy example can be replicated using all sorts of variations, for example, a change in the days of trade receivables and/or payables, or days of inventories, and produce the same effects.

The example we just discussed shows how a firm can compete by choosing its level of working capital. Firms that choose to have a low level of working capital, relying mostly on short-term debt and issuing long-term capital only when required, might capture some extra profitability as these firms are never overcapitalized; that is, they avoid holding idle cash. However, this is sustainable if the need for funds does not appear during a period in which the market is illiquid; if that does happen, the firm might not be able to finance growth (through financing of FNOs) and hence might lose competitive position against more capitalized competitors. The opposite position is one in which a firm has excess long-term financing (either long-term debt or equity). This firm is likely paying a high cost of capital for its financing, but that high cost buys the firm flexibility in the event that it needs extra financing to support its FNOs. Such a firm would be able to obtain extra profits from predation in periods (or countries) in which its less conservative competitors are forced into financial distress due to cash shortages that cannot be financed.

This discussion suggests that, in some markets, securing high levels of working capital with large levels of long-term debt or equity financing, or by developing an ongoing relationship with the capital markets, facilitates access to adequate financing and can be used to attack a competitor's market position. This is especially valuable for firms operating in countries with unstable financial environments in which access to financing is usually severely curtailed, and is especially important in those cases in which FNOs are extremely difficult to forecast and control. In other words, firms knowing the market and their competitors' strengths and weaknesses might anticipate these opportunities by setting a more conservative working capital policy, which leaves them in a position to predate on their competitors' competitive position.

Note that this discussion has implications for how firms located in developed economies with good access to liquid and efficient capital markets should treat their subsidiaries in emerging markets. Some firms treat such subsidiaries as stand-alone firms, requiring that they obtain their own financing from the market without any support from headquarters. Other firms pass on to their subsidiaries financing obtained under more favorable terms by the headquarters. Obviously, the first approach leaves the subsidiary in the same situation as a local firm, with a potential disadvantage versus competitors with better access to sources of capital. In such a case, at least part of the value of being part of a global company would be lost. A plausible explanation for such an arrangement might be that headquarters believes that financial markets correctly evaluate subsidiaries' financial risk, and hence that they consequently offer a fair-market financial contract. In contrast, if local financial markets are not assumed to be able to correctly evaluate firms' risk, that is, if the (informed) headquarters is assumed to understand its subsidiary better than the (uninformed) market, it would be in headquarters' best interest to finance the subsidiary. In this case, the subsidiary would be in better competitive shape compared to its competitors, especially if they are local firms or stand-alone subsidiaries of multinational firms. The major drawback of this policy is the potential agency cost of the strategy: under these conditions (i.e., substantial financial slack and potentially low controls due to being an overseas subsidiary), some managers might have an incentive to relax their cost controls and be tempted to spend more money than they would have spent if they were part of a stand-alone financially constrained subsidiary. In sum, both approaches have positive and negative consequences, and the decision as to which approach to follow will need to consider factors such as the competitiveness of the overseas firm's industry, the volatility of the firm's FNOs and the ability to forecast and manage them, and the ability to control managerial deviations from proposed strategies.

To summarize, the objective of these paragraphs was to show how firms can use working capital management as a competitive weapon to compete in their industrial sectors by setting the level of working capital after forecasting FNOs. Most of the discussion focuses on the case in which a firm is unable to finance its FNOs due to limited availability of financial capital (i.e., inefficient capital markets).

The discussion on the competitive advantage of using this approach can be extrapolated almost without change to the case of firms that have a seasonal business. Setting an adequate level of working capital is extremely important to compete in seasonal industries.[7]

More important, firms that understand these tools in a comprehensive way can better manage their industrial structure, and might even be able to change the rules of the game. Dell is a great case in this point. Dell competes in an industry in which competitors need to finance large FNO positions. These firms typically need to have large inventory balances, and they need to finance powerful clients. Dell decided from the beginning, however, to start with a completely different paradigm, breaking the rules of the industry and finding a way to sell computers that required virtually no investment in current assets (almost no inventories, and a large portion of their sales are made with ex ante payment). Moreover, since the firm managed to work special deals with suppliers, it actually has negative FNOs, which causes its growth to be self-sustained from the current assets standpoint. Thus, understanding the basics of working capital management and integrating this information on industry dynamics and business strategy can help managers compete at a different standard.

## CONCLUSION

In this chapter, we reviewed the use of working capital management as a strategic tool. We started by discussing the importance of taking working capital into account at the strategic planning stage. In particular, we stressed the importance of conducting a careful forecast of current assets and their respective financial needs; such forecasts are critical to making sure that the firm can obtain sufficient financing to sustain its plan. Next, we discussed the importance of working capital management at the execution stage. In the third part of the chapter, we illustrated how working capital management can be used to make operational decisions. The last part of this chapter focused on how firms can use working capital policies to compete. While current assets and FNOs are difficult for management to control, as they are sensitive to market trends, firms can choose between aggressive and conservative working capital policies in financing their FNOs.

We explained how more conservative financing strategies might lead to lower returns during normal times, but they also allow firms greater access to financial capital than their competitors during tight markets, and hence they provide firms the potential to outperform competitors that may face limits to financing future growth opportunities. Additionally, we showed that by considering the management of working capital during the strategic planning phase, firms can modify their FNOs in ways that might allow them to compete with lower financing requirements.

# 11

# Working Capital Financing Costs

As we explained in prior chapters, working capital can be interpreted as the portion of long-term financing (i.e., long-term debt and equity) that the firm uses to finance its operating investment. Working capital can also be thought of as the short-term assets financed by long-term capital.

After discussing the definition and correct interpretation of working capital and financial needs for operation, we dedicated much of this book to their main components as well as criteria that can help the manager choose an appropriate working capital management policy. We now turn to the financing costs associated with working capital. Given that we have identified its two main components, namely, long-term debt and equity financing, we will begin by focusing on the costs associated with these separate sources of funds. We will then combine these costs using the concept of weighted average cost of capital (WACC).[1]

Note that this average financing cost is relevant to a number of strategic decisions, including capital budgeting, corporate valuation, corporate restructuring, value creation, incentives, and contract design. However, because this book aims to help the manager understand the role of working capital and in turn set an optimal working capital management policy, a thorough analysis of such decisions is well outside the scope of this book. Nonetheless, the basic introduction on cost of capital estimation to follow should be a very useful foundation for further study of this key concept.

## LONG-TERM SOURCES OF FUNDS

While the two basic sources of long-term financing are long-term debt and equity, a variety of instruments can fall within these two categories. However, given that the basic intuition for establishing the various instruments' costs is similar within the two categories, we focus here only on long-term financial debt in general, and on common equity, where we abstract from special sources of funds such as convertibles, warrants, preferred equity, and the like, as such particulars are outside the scope of this book.

### Different Sources of Funds, Different Risks

There is a big difference between an investor who provides funds via a debt contract and an investor who finances the firm via equity. To see this, it is helpful to turn to an income statement.

One of the first things we may notice is that the financial creditor (or debt holder) receives its compensation (interest payments) before the owner (or equity holder) is compensated (dividends); that is, debt is paid *first*. Such seniority in claims suggests that debt has lower risk than equity. But that doesn't mean that debt is risk free. So what kind of risk is embedded in a debt contract? The main risk of debt is the risk of not being paid back, which is referred to as *default* risk. In the event of default, debt holders face uncertainty with respect to whether they will receive a large or a small part of their claim.[2] Figure 11.1 illustrates this point.

On the compensation side, however, debt holders are not paid more if the business does well. Rather, interest payments are paid according to

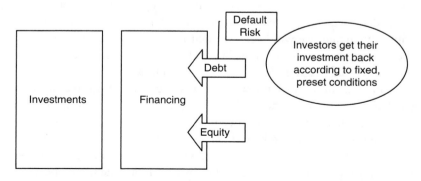

**Figure 11.1.** Debt Contract

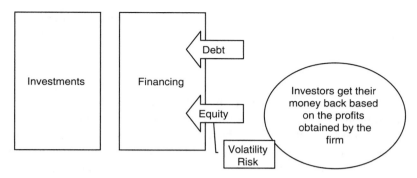

**Figure 11.2.** Equity Contract

the terms of the debt holder's contract. Such payments may be fixed or, alternatively, the contract may tie interest payments to floating rates, which certainly vary over time; but it is important to notice that this does not make the compensation business dependant: interest expenses do not depend on the outcome of the business itself, just on both the amount of money lent and the interest rate set for each particular contract (which may be fixed or floating).

In contrast to debt contracts, equity contracts are paid *last*; moreover, their return depends on how well the business is doing. So, what is the risk associated with holding equity? Do equity holders face default risk? In short, no, as equity holders are not promised any specific amount of money in return for their investment—where there is no *promise*, there is no *default*. But equity does carry *volatility* risk, which is connected to the uncertainty about the business outcome: investors may earn a lot of money if the company does well, or lose their entire investment if the business does poorly. Figure 11.2 summarizes these aspects of an equity holder's contract.

Now that we understand the main risks associated with debt and equity contracts, we can estimate the appropriate return for each of these sources of funds.

## THE COST OF DEBT

The basic intuition for determining the required return on any source of funds comes from the fundamental equation presented in Chapter 1. Given that all potential investors can invest their money in a risk-free investment,[3] they will only invest in a particular company or project if it offers them the risk-free return (the *basic* opportunity cost) plus *fair* compensation for the additional risk they assume. Thus, if we let $K_d$

denote the cost of long-term financial debt, the fundamental equation would be:

$$K_d = R_f + Risk\ Premium.$$

According to the discussion at the end of the previous section, the risk premium on a debt contract should be determined mainly by the risk of default. To evaluate this risk and translate it into a spread (the return over the basis given by the risk-free rate), banks or risk analysts evaluate a number of firm characteristics that are linked to the firm's probability of default (e.g., interest coverage ratio, cash flow generation over total debt, operating income over sales, long-term debt over capital, etc.) to estimate the cash flow generation and payment capacity of each firm. Based on the resulting estimates, a bank will set a certain spread that will be charged on funds lent to the firm. Similarly, rating agency analysts will assign a *rating* to each potential prospect, according to which investors will require a certain spread over the risk-free return—the higher the rating is, the lower the spread.[4] Therefore, the cost of debt can be summarized as follows:

$$K_d = R_f + Spread.$$

Before moving on to consider the equity cost of capital, it is worth saying a few words about what is behind this credit spread. The main driver behind the spread can be easier to see if we think about the bond market rather than the banking system. Bond spreads have two fundamental components: the probability of default and the recovery value. Thus, as we suggested earlier, lenders typically care about two things: are they going to get their money back, and, if not in full, how much can they expect to receive?

## THE COST OF EQUITY

Turning to the cost of equity, recall from Chapter 1 that this cost can be expressed as follows:

$$K_e = R_f + Equity\ Risk\ Premium.$$

The question that now arises is: how do we estimate the *equity risk premium*? Is it comparable to the risk premium on debt (i.e., the credit spread)? This does not seem very likely. As we showed in the first section, debt and equity are associated with totally different types of risk. It seems reasonable to expect that the ways of compensating different risks will themselves differ.

So, what do we know about equity that can help us determine its premium? Previously we explained that equity risk is related to volatility. Therefore, we might expect that the higher the volatility is, the higher the equity risk premium. What we need is an acceptable measure of volatility. The most common measures of volatility come from statistics: *variance* and *standard deviation*. Both the variance and the standard deviation of firms' returns represent the degree of dispersion of those returns with respect to their average value.[5] This gives us a "spread" on which to base our measure of the risk premium. But can we now simply say that the cost of equity should be directly proportional to these metrics? Is there anything missing?

If we compensate equity holders for the total dispersion observed in a [...] :tric proportional to the stan- [...] ssuming that equity holders [...] 'e know, investors are able to [...] iks by investing in assets that [...] ligned, patterns. It therefore [...] an this total dispersion mea- [...] (still connected to volatility) [...] 'rs diversify their portfolios; [...] uld not care about the total [...] the nondiversifiable portion [...] ich a measure? Yes! [...] liversifiable *quantity* of risk [...] lled *beta* (β). To understand [...] discussion in simple terms, [...] . More specifically, imagine [...] :sentative of the whole mar- [...] ...nk of him or her as invested in a fund that replicates the market index, the S&P500). Now let's assume that this investor wants to estimate how much of a return he or she should demand for a given investment in the equity of, say, Company A. At this point in our example, we need to take a small detour.

We know that, every day, the prices in the stock market move up and down. The volatility of the whole market should be a good measure of the overall risk in the market, a risk that investor cannot diversify anywhere else. This risk needs to be compensated, of course; the compensation on such risk is called the *market risk premium*. Building on this, how much more compensation should be expected by an investor in Company A? Well, if the volatility of the stock returns of Company A amplifies the

volatility of the returns on the market (both up and down), then investors should expect Company A to pay a risk premium that is higher than
the market risk premium. If, in contrast, the volatility of the stock returns
of Company A attenuates market movements, then it would be fair for
investors to receive a premium on Company A stock that is somewhat
lower than the market risk premium. A firm's *beta* represents the sensitivity of a firm's returns to the volatility of market returns: firms whose
returns amplify market volatility have a beta higher than one, and firms
whose returns attenuate market volatility have a beta lower than one.
Based on this discussion, the expected return on a firm's equity can be
captured by the following formula:

$$K_e = R_f + \beta \times Market\ Risk\ Premium.^6$$

We now encounter a familiar problem: in estimating the cost of equity,
we need to estimate each of its *components*. The first component of interest is the market risk premium; we need an estimate of the market risk
premium that represents what investors consider to be fair compensation
for investing in the market portfolio. Since, as usual, it is difficult to build
a forward-looking estimate of this number, we typically rely on historic
averages. More specifically, we look at how much extra return (over the
risk-free investment) the overall market has paid in the past by evaluating
the spread between the market and the risk-free return, over time, and
estimating an average figure. The resulting figure is an estimate of the
premium that is supported by historic data.[7]

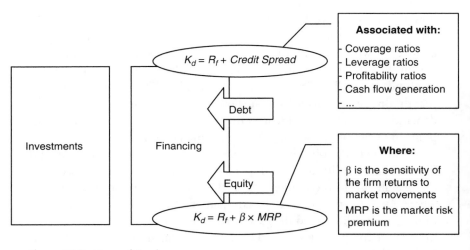

**Figure 11.3.** Costs of Funds

Further details on how to calculate the components of the cost of equity correctly are outside the scope of this book. We note, however, that in practice the manager will probably not need to estimate each of the components himself or herself. The trickiest component, beta, can be bought from market data providers such as Bloomberg, Standard and Poor's, and the like.[8] Other components can be obtained from standard market information available from more specialized sources.

Figure 11.3 summarizes our discussion so far on the cost of funds. We now are ready to combine these costs using the concept of the weighted average cost of capital.

## THE WEIGHTED AVERAGE COST OF CAPITAL

As we have previously noted, the weighted average cost of capital is simply the (weighted) average cost of a firm's sources of financing (here, long-term debt and common equity). But note that given that interest expenses are deductible at the corporate level, the relevant cost of debt is not simply the cost of debt, $K_d$, discussed above, but the after-tax cost of debt, that is, $K_d \times (1 - t)$. Thus, the formula for estimating WACC is:

$$WACC = \frac{D}{D+E} \times K_d \times (1-t) + \frac{E}{D+E} \times K_e.$$

Given the scope of the book, we conclude our discussion of this topic here. We simply emphasize that the question of how much equity and how much debt a firm should include in its capital structure is a separate subject of interest in corporate finance. The related discussion is long, and is not very conclusive so far.

## CONCLUSION

In this chapter, we discussed the main costs associated with the different sources of a firm's funds. Given that working capital is financed with both long-term debt and equity, we begin by differentiating debt from equity contracts and examining the risk associated with each type of contract. We then argued that the compensation to investors for bearing risk should be different according to the type of underlying risk. Finally, we combined the cost of debt and the cost of equity into one summary figure, WACC. Our objective was not to discuss in detail how to estimate WACC, but rather to shed light on its different components so that we can get a better sense of how costly it is for a company to obtain financing through long-term debt and equity.

# 12

## Patterns in Working Capital

This last chapter is devoted to the discussion of the cross-sectional and time-series variation in working capital patterns. By understanding how working capital policies compare across firms or industries, and by analyzing how these policies evolve over time, we can better appreciate the role of a firm's working capital strategy.

As we have seen in earlier chapters, firms' optimal working capital policies are affected by several factors; some of them are exogenous, while others are endogenous to the firm. This implies that not only firm-specific factors but also industry-and country-specific factors can affect the variation in working capital practices across firms. Such factors include the firm's strength vis à vis counterparties in negotiations, the financial flexibility of the firm, the number of firms offering the service or product, the amount of demand for the service or product, and the extent to which the country in which the firm is domiciled enforces rule of law.

Additionally, a firm's working capital tends to change over time, given that the various determinants of working capital also change. For instance, the financial strength of a firm is likely to influence its ability to negotiate with commercial partners and obtain favorable terms of trade. Moreover, the financial strength of the economy, which varies over economic cycles, is also likely to be an important determinant of working capital management.

The objective of this chapter is to discuss how these factors affect a firm's financial needs for operation (FNOs), working capital, and ultimately working capital management policies.

## DIFFERENCES ACROSS COUNTRIES

The discussion in the previous chapters developed the intuition that different countries, with different economies and financial systems, should observe differences in firms' optimal working capital policies.

Firms operating in countries with larger and more stable financial systems have more opportunities to sort out any deviation in the gap between FNOs and working capital, and thus have a lower incentive to keep high levels of working capital for precautionary reasons. Therefore, firms in countries with more developed financial markets can keep working capital as low as required by the lowest level of seasonal FNOs, and can rely on short-term debt to finance the seasonal gap. This short-term debt will be refunded to the bank as soon as the FNOs decline following a seasonal peak. In the event the FNOs do not decrease all the way to their expected level, firms can always increase working capital by obtaining long-term funding from the capital markets.[1] In contrast, if a firm is undercapitalized in a country in which capital markets are not efficient, the unexpected gap will be most likely covered, if at all, with short-term debt. This poses the risk that at some point the amount of funds required would become larger than the level allowed by the bank, which could lead the firm into financial distress or even bankruptcy.

Additionally, firms located in countries with inefficient capital markets may need to rely more on suppliers' trade credit as a structural financing tool. Thus, depending on the receivables-payables balance, some suppliers will have higher FNOs simply because they need to sustain their clients for a longer period of time than otherwise similar firms in other countries.

A third way a firm's country of domicile can impact its working capital is through efficiency effects. As La Porta, Lopez-de-Silanes, Shleifer, and Vishny (1997, 2000) note, countries with less developed capital markets are usually countries with less developed institutions. In such an environment, efficiency tends to be lower. This, in turn, is likely to lead to higher FNOs. For instance, collecting receivables might be more complicated or receiving shipments from suppliers might take longer than expected, causing firms to place larger orders for precautionary reasons.[2]

In sum, sound institutional frameworks in general and capital markets in particular allow for less restrictive working capital management policies. In this case, FNOs are usually low and any gap resulting from seasonality or simple volatility can typically be funded with short-term sources of funds. In contrast, less developed legal and financial contexts may lead to higher FNOs but working capital that is set below its optimal level (given that long-term sources of funds are not available). This higher gap has to be financed with short-term debt, which, in these markets, is not always available. Empirical observations and anecdotal evidence might, in some cases, show a counterargument. In countries with a poor institutional environment and underdeveloped financial markets, some firms might try to improve their operational efficiency, decreasing their level of FNOs, in order to have a lower gap to finance.

## MACROECONOMIC CONDITIONS

### Monetary Constraints

According to the redistribution view discussed in Chapter 6, access to financing is likely to be asymmetric, and this asymmetry is likely to be higher during monetary contractions. The idea is that when cash is scarce, large firms might enjoy greater access to financing than small firms, and thus, in an attempt to obtain a commercial advantage over smaller competitors that cannot offer financing, they might have an incentive to support their clients via trade receivables. Put differently, when credit is rationed, firms with better access to financing may have an incentive to differentiate themselves from their competitors by using trade credit to support smaller, more credit-constrained clients (Meltzer, 1960). During times of monetary contraction, some firms might try to use their market power to squeeze suppliers and improve liquidity. This would cause a reduction in their FNOs and an increase in their suppliers'. In essence, monetary conditions affect both FNOs and working capital by influencing the firm's ability to obtain financing and their propensity to enter into late payments.

### Inflation

Another macroeconomic factor that might affect a firm's working capital is inflation. During periods of high inflation that economic agents believe is going to last for some time, there are likely to be effects to both FNOs and the level of working capital.

On the investment side (the FNOs), every firm has a higher incentive to collect receivables faster, since each day until collection costs more in terms of loss of value. The firm's suppliers, however, also attempt to accelerate collection of receivables. As a consequence, there is a certain tension for cash between clients and suppliers. Consider Firm ABC, as an example: while ABC's suppliers will be attempting to collect their money sooner rather than later (which would work to increase ABC's FNOs), ABC will be aiming to shorten its own collection period (which will lower the FNOs required by ABC). Obviously, the balance will depend on the ability of both sides (the supplier and the client) to enforce payment.

On the financing side of the balance sheet, the incentive to use a higher share of long-term funds decreases. Working capital is expensive in terms of cost of capital, and in the context of inflation, even more so: the risk-free threshold is now higher due to higher current and expected inflation. Under these conditions, investors increase their required returns, so firms might be reluctant to lock into long-term debt contracts at high interest rates. Further, especially if there is an expectation that inflation rates will be lower at some point in the future, firms have an incentive to issue short-term debt until market conditions allow them to refinance into longer maturities.

Note that this discussion also applies to high interest rates (not necessarily due to high inflation); high interest rates cause the same effects to FNOs and working capital as described earlier.

## Crisis

When an economy is hit by a crisis, this leads to substantial effects on both working capital policies and working capital real movements. We could analyze the impact of economic crises on each working capital determinant: cash holdings, inventories, receivables, payables, and short-term debt. Love, Preve, and Sarria-Allende (2007), for example, study the effects of financial crises on the level of credit that firms extend to their clients, as well as on the level of credit firms receive from their suppliers. In particular, the authors ask whether trade credit has a role in sustaining firms' commercial activities during times when financial markets effectively shut down. Using a sample of firms located in countries that suffered severe financial crises during the 1990s, such as Mexico, Indonesia, South Korea, Thailand, Malaysia, and the Philippines,[3] the authors look at patterns in each firm's trade credit during the crisis year, compared to precrisis and postcrisis figures. They find that trade credit tends to increase during a financial crisis, and that this increase is both economically and statistically significant. On average, firms appear to give to clients and receive from suppliers almost eight days of extra credit during times of crisis. However, the paper also shows that following a crisis, firms tend to sharply decrease trade credit to levels that are lower from those of the precrisis period. The authors find this result consistent with the redistribution view of trade credit: if trade credit typically channels credit from *stronger* to more credit-constrained firms, it is reasonable to expect that when no bank credit is available, channeling is not feasible.[4]

In sum, the significant increase in trade credit during a crisis suggests that in cases in which a sudden and severe slowdown in the economy leads the banking system to grind to a temporary halt, firms will supply increased financing in a *lender of last resort* kind of way. After this initial role, however, the level of trade financing tends to decrease on both sides of the balance sheet, probably because at some point it becomes impossible to continue such credit channeling (as there is no bank credit), and also because any over-euphoria in the precrisis period starts to be recognized and taken into account.

## FINANCIAL DISTRESS AT THE FIRM LEVEL

The situations discussed so far affect the economy as a whole. In this section, we study the effects of firm-level financial distress on working capital. More specifically, we concentrate on the effects of financial distress on the allowance and use of trade credit.

As before, we start by considering the effect of financial distress on the operating investment of the firm, that is, on its FNOs. The impact of corporate financial distress on trade receivables might be twofold. On the one hand, a firm that starts to face profitability problems will have an incentive to increase sales by offering increased financing to clients; such a step will increase its FNOs.[5] On the other hand, firms in financial distress are financially constrained and hence are likely to underinvest (Myers, 1977). These patterns of increasing investment in market share through larger trade receivables and decreasing investment in general due to financial constraints will clearly affect a firm's profitability, though in different directions, since they represent a deviation from the optimal investment policy.

In a recent paper, Molina and Preve (2009a) study the effect of financial distress on the trade receivables of U.S. companies. Using firm-level data from the Compustat database, the authors analyze the financing that firms facing financial distress extend to clients. The results show that while firms increase their trade receivables during low profitability years preceding financial distress, they decrease the level of financing to clients when they enter financial distress and start facing cash flow problems. More specifically, the paper shows that, on average, firms in financial distress decrease trade receivables by more than two days.

Interestingly, however, this result is not uniform across firms or industries. One of the main industry characteristics that affects the trade receivables of firms in distress is its level of competitiveness. Firms in more competitive industries are more likely to be forced to accept the conditions imposed by the market, while firms in more concentrated industries are more likely to be able to use trade receivables as a weapon to increase sales and market share when facing profitability problems. Following the same intuition, upon entering financial distress, these firms are more likely to be able to cut their investment in client financing without suffering strong penalties in terms of decreased sales. In contrast, a firm in an industry in which several competitors offer similar products is not likely to be able to decrease trade receivables and retain their sales volume, as their clients can easily switch suppliers and leave the firm with a lower volume of sales. Thus, it is not surprising that Molina and Preve (2009a) also show that only those firms in concentrated industries decrease trade receivables during financial distress.

In another paper, Molina and Preve (2009b) extend their prior work by analyzing the effects of financial distress on trade credit received from suppliers. That is, while in Molina and Preve (2009a) the authors analyze the investing behavior of the distressed firm, in the follow-up paper they study the effect of firms' financial distress on the credit behavior of their suppliers. They find that supplier financing increases when the firm is in financial distress. The finding that suppliers provide supplemental financial aid for firms in financial trouble is an interesting result, since most of the usual sources of financing tend to dry up when firms enter distress. Yet suppliers are typically the ones that force firms into bankruptcy if their restructuring is not successful. This makes the relation between a distressed firm and its suppliers a very complex one and an interesting subject of study.

Note that in both papers, Molina and Preve measure the cost embedded in the suboptimal trade credit behavior of firms in financial distress. The implicit assumption is that the trade credit behavior of firms not in distress is optimal, and thus when firms in distress deviate from this behavior, they enter a suboptimal investment or financing pattern that must have some associated cost. This cost represents one of the costs of financial distress that the financial literature has been seeking to identify in recent years.

Another key component of a firm's operating assets is inventory. We are not aware of any academic study that relates a firm's inventory balances to financial distress. Relying on our intuition, we expect that when a firm faces financial distress, the level of the firm's inventory is likely to decrease due to the firm trying to minimize investments and cash expenditures. The rationale is that distressed firms are less likely to buy larger quantities at a discounted price, while firms with larger levels of inventory have an incentive to sell their inventory as fast as possible to convert it into cash. However, it is difficult to draw more general conclusions about a firm's inventory balances since they are probably very closely linked to firm and industry characteristics, and each case is likely to be distinct.

In sum, we do not have a clear-cut directional prediction for the behavior of FNOs when a firm experiences financial distress; we can only predict the behavior of some of its individual components. The main reason for this is that since the behavior of FNOs is extremely firm dependent, it is difficult to draw general conclusions about them.

We now move to the financing side of the balance sheet and consider what happens to the level of working capital during financial distress. Financially distressed firms are suffering losses; the main definitions of financial distress involve negative profits.[6] When firms have negative profits, the book value of their equity starts to decline, and there is usually a good chance that the market value of equity will follow a similar pattern. This suggests that firms in financial distress that do not issue new equity are likely to exhibit a decrease in the level of their equity. Turning to long-term debt financing, unless the firm can generate expectations that lead investors to buy its long-term debt, it is unlikely that it will be able to raise long-term debt. The third component in determining a firm's working capital is its level of fixed assets. Firms in financial distress are likely to sell assets, even if the price they obtain is not the fair market price (such asset sales are called fire sales),[7] as the sale of fixed assets allows the firm to increase its working capital. In sum, financially distressed firms are likely to see a decline in the level of their long-term capital due to a decrease in both equity and long-term debt, but they are also likely to sell some fixed assets, alleviating, at least in part, the net effect on working capital. Obviously, the impact of financial distress on the level of working capital will mainly depend on firm and industry characteristics and will not be the same across firms.

Unfortunately, there are no empirical studies that analyze the effect of financial distress on the working capital policy of the firm. We hypothesize that, on average, financially distressed firms tend to observe a decrease in the level of working capital relative to FNOs, increasing the gap between the two. This would cause financially distressed firms to require more short-term financial support from banks, which would subsequently worsen their overall financial condition. However, any further predictions cannot be made with any confidence without relying on more research on the topic.

## CONCLUSION

This chapter discussed some of the patterns that we observe in working capital management over time and across firms or industries. Since this topic has not been fully considered by academic research, there is only an incomplete body of literature from which we can draw in discussing firms' behavior under different circumstances. It is our sincere hope that academics will start studying this topic in greater detail in the near future.

# Notes

## Chapter 1

1. Obviously, this classification is highly simplified. For now it is worth noting that debt holders are usually divided into banks and bond holders. At this stage, no further distinctions between investors need to be drawn.

2. Liquidity has two basic components: time (how fast a given asset can be turned into cash) and cost (how much of a loss of value is incurred in turning a given asset into cash).

3. Note that this convention may change from place to place. For example, in the United States and Latin America, the accounts are sorted by decreasing liquidity (most liquid assets at the top), whereas in Continental Europe, the sorting follows the opposite ordering, with fixed assets at the top and more liquid assets at the bottom.

4. For now we can say that if the invoice has been paid, then the payment is probably recorded as part of the firm's cash assets, and if it has not been paid, then the payment is still recorded as an asset, but in this case as trade credit to clients.

5. Note that sometimes the estimation of sales *minus* CGS is called the contribution margin. The distinction between the two concepts depends on whether the costs included in CGS are all the variable costs or just the direct costs. This distinction does not affect our analysis, however, and thus we do not dig any deeper into the nuances of CGS. As a quick reference: a variable cost is a cost that varies with the level of production, and a direct cost is a cost that can be directly imputed to a certain product or product line, regardless of whether it is fixed or variable.

6. A claim holder is somebody that holds a claim on the cash flows generated by the firm.

7. The retained earnings are expected to influence the actual value of a given stock. Therefore, the investors' return will include these two components: dividends paid and capital gains.

## Chapter 2

1. *Short-term operating liabilities* include all expenses owed to suppliers of goods and services plus taxes.

2. From Figure 2.1, we see that *capital* includes *long-term financial debt* and *equity.*

3. This is why some authors refer to these debts as *spontaneous resources;* see, for example, Faus (1997).

4. Note that $1,000 of capital, retained earnings in this case, was financing the net operating investment (FNOs = $1,000).

5. Additionally, a change in FNOs can also be induced by a change in the commercial conditions of the firm. We will discuss this point later in the chapter.

6. Even if cash is more liquid than trade receivables and inventory, we reverse the order of the presentation because of the greater relevance of the latter two items to working capital decisions.

7. Some firms also classify goods in process as part of their inventory accounts. We will discuss this point in greater detail in Chapter 6.

8. For instance, this average calculation suppresses the fact that it depends on the different types of inventory held, the added value of the products held in inventory, and so forth.

9. At this stage, we are loose with respect to the definition of cost. We discuss this issue in greater detail in Chapter 6.

10. This might be due to the common misunderstanding where working capital is taken to be a short-term concept, as we discussed earlier in this chapter.

11. See Porter (1980).

12. This is true in the case of efficient financial markets, where a firm is assumed to get the appropriate financing at the correct price. In the case of emerging financial markets, however, long-term debt financing might not be available at any price and equity markets might not exist. In such markets, working capital might not be an item over which management makes a choice.

## Chapter 3

1. We discuss the impact of poor working capital policies in Chapter 11.

2. Later we will describe the two main objectives of this practice, namely, ensuring necessary liquidity and avoiding interest rate risk.

3. This choice is available to many seasonal businesses, except for those that produce perishable goods and most businesses that provide services.

4. For a precise definition and more detailed explanation, refer back to Chapter 2.

5. See Myers and Majluf (1984); Jensen and Meckling (1976); and a large group of subsequent studies.

6. Assuming a typical upward-sloping yield curve.

7. As suggested by Genoni and Zurita (2003).

8. While keeping a higher inventory of raw materials reduces the probability of stockouts during the production process, a higher level of inventory of final goods facilitates sales and increases service quality by reducing the probability of customers walking out without the desired product (see Fazzari and Petersen, 1993).

9. In fact, extending credit periods allows liquidity-constrained customers to place (more) orders.

10. This scenario is often overlooked when people fail to differentiate between working capital and FNOs.

## Chapter 4

1. The tax shield results from deductable interest expenses.

2. We will briefly comment on this when talking about financing costs in Chapter 11.

3. We have included them here, however, to clarify the usual misinterpretation.

4. Hodrick and Moulton (2009).

5. The use of 360 is customary. The year, however, has a total of 365 days, so that could be another option. Additionally, some companies may be interested in scaling annual figures by computing only business days. The key issue is to look at the precise definition before interpreting or comparing numbers.

6. Since, as we mentioned earlier, sales are realized throughout the year while inventory is measured at a given point in time, one should estimate the latter by using some sort of averaging (either by using beginning- and end-of-year figures or by using quarterly or monthly statements, depending on the firm's exposure to seasonality).

7. Value creation can be evaluated by comparing the actual shareholder return (ROE) with his or her expected return (which basically depends on the level of risk he or she is facing). Therefore, even when debt increases ROE (in cases where ROA > Kd), it will only create value if it does not increase the required/expected return proportionally. This evaluation relates to Modigliani and Miller's contribution (1958, 1963), but it goes beyond the scope of this chapter and, indeed, book.

8. For simplicity, we present our analysis here using the formula that applies to a world with no taxes. Incorporating taxes does not change the analysis in any substantial way; as can be observed in the corresponding equation presented later, doing so simply requires using the after-tax ROA and the after-tax cost of debt [which should be computed as $K_d \times (1 - t)$].

If we take the formula for ROE and multiply and divide the right-hand side (RHS) by net assets, we get:

$$ROE = \frac{Net\ Income}{Net\ Assets} \times \frac{Net\ Assets}{Equity}.$$

Now, given that in a world with no taxes, net income is equal to EBIT minus interest expenses (INT), we can write ROE as:

$$ROE = (\frac{EBIT - INT}{Net\ Assets}) \times \frac{Net\ Assets}{Equity}.$$

Once we apply the distributive property and both multiply and divide the second term by total debt, we obtain:

$$ROE = \frac{EBIT}{Net\ Assets} \times \frac{Net\ Assets}{Equity} - \frac{INT}{Debt} \times \frac{Debt}{Net\ Assets} \times \frac{Net\ Assets}{Equity}.$$

Letting $K_d$ represent the firm's cost of debt, and replacing net assets by its equal, we can write:

$$ROE = ROA \times \frac{Debt + Equity}{Equity} - K_d \times \frac{Debt}{Equity}.$$

which, reorganizing terms, generates the expression suggested in the text.

This same formula, in a world with taxes, is given by:

$$ROE = ROA + \frac{Debt}{Equity}(ROA - K_d \times (1-t)),$$

where ROA is now the after-tax return on assets and $t$ is the effective tax rate.

9. The two objectives follow the same approach. Specifically, when we analyze a firm's performance over time, we look at the firm's information across at least two or three consecutive years. When we compare the firm's performance to that of its competitors, each column in the analysis represents information about one of the firms under consideration, as reported at a particular point in time.

10. Even though, strictly speaking, we are talking about RONA (i.e., using net assets as the scaling factor), we will continue working with the expression ROA, since it is the most common name people use.

11. It is important to notice that, in order to estimate the amount covered by equity financing, one needs to forecast the income statement, which will give us a sense of the estimated retained earnings.

12. Remember that in exchange for the market price (of a stock), one is entitled to the complete series of future expected cash flows.

## Chapter 5

1. See Bates, Kahle, and Stulz (2006); Himmelberg, Love, and Sarria-Allende (2008); and Preve (2009).

2. See Bates, Kahle, and Stultz (2006) for a complete reference.

3. See references mentioned in footnote #1.

4. Most of the empirical studies analyzing corporate cash holdings considered cash to be the sum of effective cash plus marketable securities. In this chapter, however, we present some of the basic frameworks that take cash to be a more rigorous term.

5. Even though when considering transaction demand we typically differentiate between cash and marketable securities, most studies analyzing corporate cash holdings use a broader definition of cash, which consolidates these two items.

6. Baumol (1952).

7. Himmelberg et al (2008) show that firms that have higher material and labor expenses, which presumably must be paid in cash, have higher cash-to-asset ratios.

8. Later in this chapter, we discuss how different cash conversion cycles (related to the actual rhythm of collections and payments) influence corporate cash holding policies.

9. Miller and Orr (1966).

10. In the case of private firms, it is frequently the case that the firm's financial slack is directly maintained by shareholders: those shareholders who know the company's risk may choose to maintain certain levels of cash to hedge that risk. In such cases, the opportunity cost of holding highly liquid assets is borne by the shareholders, not by the firm. There are risks associated with this strategy, however. On the one hand, shareholders face the risk associated with coordinating among themselves on the necessity of capitalizing the firm. On the other hand, under this strategy, third parties may not perceive the liquidity cushion and hence may require alternative warranties (such as the Comfort Letters many banks require when lending money to private firms).

11. See Himmelberg et al. (2008).

12. For a complete reference, see Opler, Pinkowitz, Stulz, and Williamson (1999); and Bates et al. (2006).

13. Some firms have established lockbox systems to accelerate check processing. Lockbox systems consist of setting a post office box that, controlled by the firm's bank, facilitates the process of collecting and depositing customers' payments.

## Chapter 6

1. Petersen and Rajan (1997), Table I.

2. Molina and Preve (2009a) estimate this cost as 13% of the firm's value.

3. According to the previous discussion, credit risk is the possibility that the commercial credit might be not repaid according to the originally scheduled terms.

4. See Altman (1993) and Pascale (2009) for more information on the model and extensions to several countries and industries.

5. One home-based example of contingent payment would be insurance against fire accidents. If you pay for such insurance, you have the right to receive an agreed upon payment in the event your house is destroyed by fire. Two interesting examples of credit derivatives for the case of commercial credit are the credit default put and the credit default swap. Their detailed explanation is beyond the scope of this book, but can be found in most risk management books.

6. We say short-term debt because the life of these assets is usually 6 to 12 months.

7. Obviously, if sales are observed quarterly, the denominator of the fraction should be 90, and so on.

## Chapter 7

1. Note that a finished good of one firm can be part of the raw materials in the production process of another firm, of which the former is a supplier, so these terms are *relative* terms.

2. The money tied up in overinvestment in inventory can also be interpreted as having an opportunity cost.

3. We refer the interested reader to standard accounting textbooks for discussions on other methodologies and related references.

4. Given that investment in inventory is more flexible (adjustable) than fixed investment, its associated risk (i.e., cost of capital) is likely smaller than that of fixed investment. However, recent research shows that this flexibility advantage is more than offset by the higher depreciation rate of inventory. See Jones and Tuzel (2009).

5. Ross, Westerfield, and Jordan (2001).

6. To review the mathematical details of the minimization process, we refer the reader to any book on calculus.

## Chapter 8

1. This number is calculated using data on U.S. public corporations from the Compustat database between 1978 and 2000.

2. To calculate this figure, we use the following equation:

$$(1 + 0.02)^{\frac{360}{20}} = (1 + i),$$

which allows us to move from a 20-day rate to an annual rate. Solving for $I$, we get:

$$i = 42.82\%.$$

For more information on this equivalence, please refer to your favorite finance textbook.

3. It is interesting to notice that this condition does not change over time (whereas interest rates show significant change).

4. See Smith (1987), Mian and Smith (1992), Biais and Gollier (1997), Frank and Maksimovic (2004), Deloof and Jegers (1996), Emery and Nayar (1998), Lee and Stowe (1993), Long, Malitz, and Ravid (1993), and Burkart and Ellingsen (2003).

5. See Cunat (2000) and Wilner (2000).

6. See Molina and Preve (2009b) for a more detailed description.

7. See page 1072 in Altman (1984).

8. Globe Newspaper Company—*The Boston Globe*—Kimberley Blanton—December 4, 1997, Thursday, City Edition.

9. Purchases can be derived from the following expression:

$$CGS = Initial\ Inventory + Purchases - Final\ Inventories.$$

Solving for purchases, we get:

$$Purchases = CGS + Final\ Inventories - Initial\ Inventories.$$

10. Remember that this concept is equivalent to the investment in current assets that is *not* financed by suppliers or any other source of operating source of funds (such as accrued taxes and wages).

## Chapter 9

1. Remember that working capital is the portion of current assets financed with long-term resources, that is, with long-term debt and equity.

2. This is justified by the trade-off between the upward-sloping yield curve (which makes long-term financing more expensive) and the downturn and rollover risks associated with nonpermanent sources of funds. This argument is presented in Chapter 3.

3. Information asymmetry plays a very important role in corporate finance theory. We are in a better condition to understand managerial decisions if we recognize the importance of information levels in the interaction between *informed* managers and *uninformed* investors. Managers use their decisions to convey information to the investors.

4. For a more detailed argument, see Danisevska (2002).

5. This has been documented by Broner, Lorenzoni, and Schmukler (2004), at the country level, where firms have been found to borrow short-term financing, influenced by the high-risk premium the market assigns to their long-term debt alternatives.

6. Demirguc-Kunt and Maksimovic (1996).

7. Schmukler and Vesperoni (2000).

8. Interest rates can be fixed or floating; the latter are typically quoted in relation to some relevant reference rate, such as the London Interbank offered rate (LIBOR).

9. A complete discussion of these techniques can be found in the literature dealing with factoring and structured financing.

10. The SPV is a separate legal entity that takes possession of the goods, issues the corresponding asset-backed securities, and advances the money to the firm.

11. See Mann (2000).

12. Investment-grade securities are those rated BBB or higher.

13. Typically, a business plan needs to be presented and approved.

14. See Hart and Moore (1998); and Bolton and Scharfstein (1996).

15. Again, see Bolton and Scharfstein (1996).

16. More specifically, Diamond and Rajan (2000) show this at the country level.

## Chapter 10

1. See Fraile and Romero (2003).

2. To compute this figure, we need to obtain the daily level of sales ($55,154 / 360 = $153.21) and then multiply it by the nu mber of days that the firm is planning to finance its clients. For example, if the company gives clients an average of 16.2 days to pay their bills (as it has been doing in the recent past), we obtain $153.21 × 16.2 = $2,481. This calculation can be done for any estimated number of days of client financing.

3. For simplicity, we are assuming that costs do not increase. In case they do, the logic follows as well.

4. Obviously, it might be difficult to consider a net divestiture of assets in the case of a growing firm (unless it had some nonperforming assets to sell).

5. This might happen if a client has a well-defined schedule of required deliveries that the supplier knows in advance.

6. The FNOs for firm XYZ are calculated as follows: $((48,000/360) \times 10) + ((40,000/360) \times 15) - ((40,000/360) \times 30) = -333.33$.

7. Please refer to Chapter 3 for a detailed discussion on seasonality, growth, and working capital management.

## Chapter 11

1. To be more precise, WACC may consider not only the cost of long-term debt and equity but also the cost of any kind of structural short-term financial debt (many businesses rely on short-term debt as a structural—even if seasonal—form of financing).

2. Note that uncertainty is not the same thing as risk, but it is sufficiently similar for our focus here.

3. This is true only for investments in a *hard currency*; in an emerging market, a risk-free investment may be impossible to find in some local currencies.

4. Ratings are usually classified into two broad categories: investment-grade instruments (having ratings of BBB or higher) and non—investment-grade instruments, or speculative debt (having ratings lower than BBB).

5. The statistical formulas for both expressions are available in any textbook and on several websites. We focus here only on the intuition.

6. This formula is the most basic result of the capital asset pricing model (CAPM). The reader can read extensively about this method in any corporate finance manual.

7. There is some debate among academics about the most sensible way to estimate the market risk premium. For instance, some academics and practitioners prefer to use geometric historic averages, while others prefer to take an arithmetic mean. Also, there is no agreement about how long a period should be considered in taking the corresponding average; in our view, given the volatility that characterizes equity markets, any sensible figure needs to be evaluated over a relatively long time span. Further details on this issue can be found in any corporate finance manual.

8. Note that comparables' betas need to be adjusted according to leverage ratios. Again, this is very well explained in typical corporate finance manuals.

## Chapter 12

1. This permanent increase in FNOs could be due to a permanent increase in sales or due to structural changes in trade conditions.

2. This inefficiency might be especially troublesome for firms that have large levels of foreign trade, as such firms may need to rely on customs efficiency to import goods or on an efficient banking system to make payments to foreign suppliers or collect payments from foreign customers.

3. The authors were not able to include firms from Russia, Argentina, and Brazil—countries that also experienced economic crises during the period analyzed. The reason is that the research design required a three-year precrisis period and at least a one-year post-crisis period, and these countries did not have a clean precrisis and/or postcrisis period during the sample period under consideration.

4. These results might suffer from a sample selection bias. The dataset used for the paper, World Scope Data, only captures the largest firms in each economy; therefore, the behavior captured in the study is biased to the more dominant firms in each country. As a consequence, smaller firms are not directly captured in the study, but the effect of a crisis on their patterns of trade credit is only considered in an indirect way—as trading partners of the large firms observed in the dataset.

5. This is precisely one of the findings in Petersen and Rajan (1997).

6. The usual measures of financial distress are those introduced by Asquith, Gertner, and Scharfstein (1994) and DeAngelo and DeAngelo (1990). The first relies on the comparison of equity before interest and taxes (EBIT) and interest payments, while the second uses net losses.

7. See Pulvino (1998).

# References

Altman, E., 1968, "Financial Ratios, Discriminant Analysis and the Prediction of Corporate Bankruptcy," *Journal of Finance* 23, 4, 589–609.

Altman, E., 1984, "A Further Investigation on the Bankruptcy Cost Question," *Journal of Finance* 39, 1067–1089.

Altman, E., 1993, *Corporate Financial Distress and Bankruptcy*, Second Edition, John Wiley and Sons, New York, NY.

Andrade, G., and S. Kaplan, 1998, "How Costly Is Financial (Not Economic) Distress? Evidence from Highly Leveraged Transactions That Became Distressed," *Journal of Finance* 53, 1443–1493.

Asquith, P., R. Gertner, and D. Sharfstein, 1994, "Anatomy of a Financial Distress: An Examination of Junk-bond Issuers," *Quarterly Journal of Economics* 109, 625–658.

Bates, T., K. Kahle, and R. Stulz, 2006, "Why Do U.S. Firms Hold so Much More Cash Than They Used To?" *NBER Working Paper Series* 12534.

Baumol, W.S., 1952, "The Transactions Demand for Cash: An Inventory Approach," *Quarterly Journal of Economics* 66 November, 545–556.

Baxter, N.D., 1967, "Leverage, Risk of Ruin and the Cost of Capital," *Journal of Finance* 22, 395–403.

Biais, B., and C. Gollier, 1997, "Trade Credit and Credit Rationing," *Review of Financial Studies* 10(4), 903–937.

Bolton, P., and D. Scharfstein, 1996, "Optimal Debt Structure and the Number of Creditors," *Journal of Political Economy* 104, 1.

Brennan, M., V. Maksimovic, and J. Zechner, 1988, "Vendor Financing," *Journal of Finance* 43, 1127–1141.

Broner, F., G. Lorenzoni, and S. Schmukler, 2004, "Why Do Emerging Economies Borrow Short Term?" *World Bank Policy Research Working Paper* 3389.

Burkart, M., and T. Ellingsen, 2002, "In-kind Finance," *Stockholm School of Economics Working Papers Series.*

Cunat, V., 2000, "Suppliers as Debt Collectors and Insurance Providers," *FMG Discussion Paper Series* DP365.

Danisevska, P., June 2002, "Is Debt Maturity Determined by Asymmetric Information about Short-Term or Long-Term Earnings?" *EFMA 2002 London Meetings.*

DeAngelo, H., and L. DeAngelo, 1990, "Dividend Policy and Financial Distress: An Empirical Investigation of Troubled NYSE Firms," *Journal of Finance* 45, 1415–1431.

Deloof, M., and M. Jegers, 1996, "Trade Credit, Product Quality, and Intragroup Trade: Some European Evidence" *Financial Management* 25(3), 956–968.

Demirguc-Kunt, A., and V. Maksimovic, 1996, "Institutions, Financial Markets and Firm Debt Maturity," *World Bank Policy Research Working Paper* 1686.

Diamond, D., and R. Rajan, 2000, "Banks, Short Term and Financial Crisis: Theory, Policy Implications and Applications," *CRSP Working Paper* 518.

Emery, G., 1984, "A Pure Financial Explanation for Trade Credit," *Journal of Financial and Quantitative Analysis* 19, 271–285.

Emery, G., and N. Nandkumar, 1998, "Product Quality and Payment Policy," *Review of Quantitative Finance and Accounting* 10, 269–284.

Fama, E.F. and K.R. French, 1997, "Industry Cost of Equity," *Journal of Financial Economics* 43, 153–193.

Faus, J., 1997, *Finanzas Operativas: lo que todo directivo debería saber*, Ediciones Folio Biblioteca IESE, Ediciones Folio, Barcelona, Spain.

Fazzari, S. M. and B. C. Petersen, 1993, "*Working Capital and Fixed Investment: New Evidence on Financing Constraints*," *RAND Journal of Economics*, The RAND Corporation, vol. 24(3), 328–342, Autumn.

Ferris, J.S. 1981, "A Transaction Theory of Trade Credit Use," *Quarterly Journal of Economics* 96(2), 243–270.

Fraile, G. and V. Romero, 2003, Razzani-Vera S.A., IAE Business School Case FZ-C-035-IA-1-e.

Frank, M., and V. Macsimovic, 2004, "Trade Credit, Adverse Selection, and Collateral," *University of Maryland, Working Paper.*

Genoni, G., and S. Zurita, 2003, "Capital de Trabajo, Gestión de Tesorería y Evaluación de Compañías," *Universidad Adolfo Ibáñez Working Paper* 44.

Giannetti, Mariassunta, Mike Burkart and Tore Ellingsen, 2008, What You See is What You Lend? Explaining Trade Credit Contracts, *The Review of Financial Studies, forthcoming.* Hart, O., and J. Moore, 1998, "Default and Renegotiation: A Dynamic Model of Debt," *Quarterly Journal of Economics* 113, 1.

Himmelberg, C., I. Love, and V. Sarria-Allende, 2008, "A Cash in Advance Model of the Firm: Theory and Evidence," *Unpublished Manuscript.*

Hodrick, L.S., and P.C. Moulton, 2009, "Liquidity: Considerations of a Portfolio Manager," *Financial Management* Spring, 59–74.

Jaffee, D.M., 1968, "Credit Rationing and the Commercial Loan Market," Unpublished Ph.D. Dissertation, MIT.

Jensen, M., and W. Meckling, 1976, "Theory of the Firm: Managerial Behavior, Agency Costs, and Ownership Structure," *Journal of Financial Economics* 3(4), 305–360.

Jones, C., and S. Tuzel, 2009, "Inventory Investment and the Cost of Capital," *Working Paper Series SSRN*.

La Porta, R., F. Lopez-de-Silanes, A. Shleifer, and R. Vishny, 1997, "Legal Determinants of External Finance," *Journal of Finance 52, issue 3, 1131–1150*.

La Porta, R., F. Lopez-de-Silanes, A. Shleifer, and R. Vishny, 2000, "Investors Protection and Corporate Governance," *Journal of Financial Economics*.

Lee, Y.W., and J.D. Stowe, 1993, "Product Risk, Asymmetric Information, and Trade Credit," *Journal of Financial and Quantitative Analysis* 28, 285–300.

Lindsay, R., and A. Sametz, 1967, *Financial Management: An Analytical Approach*, Revised Edition. Homewood, IL: Richard D. Irwin.

Long, M., I. Malitz, and A. Ravid, 1993, "Trade Credit, Quality Guarantees, and Product Marketability," *Financial Management* 22, 117–127.

Love, I., L.A. Preve, and V. Sarria-Allende, 2007, "Trade Credit and Bank Credit: Evidence from Recent Financial Crises," *Journal of Financial Economics* 83, 453–469.

Mann, R., 2000, "The Role of Letters of Credit in Payment Transactions," *Michigan Law Review* 99, 2494.

Meltzer, A.H., 1960, "Mercantile Credit, Monetary Policy, and Size of Firms," *Review of Economics and Statistics* 42(4), 429–437.

Mian, S.L., and C.W. Smith Jr., 1992, "Accounts Receivable Management Policy: Theory and Evidence," *Journal of Finance* 47, 169–200.

Miwa, Yoshiro, and J. Mark Ramseyer, 2008, "The Implications of Trade Credit for Bank Monitoring: Suggestive Evidence," *Journal of Economics & Management Strategy*, Volume 17, Number 2, 317–343.

Modigliani, F., and M.H. Miller, 1958, "The Cost of Capital, Corporate Finance and the Theory of Investment," *American Economic Review* 48, 261–297.

Modigliani, F., and M.H. Miller, 1963, "Corporate Income Taxes and the Cost of Capital: A Correction," *American Economic Review* 53, 433–443.

Molina, C., and L.A. Preve, 2009a, "Trade Receivables Policy of Distressed Firms and Its Effect on the Cost of Financial Distress," *Financial Management*, Fall, 663–686.

Molina, C., and L.A. Preve, 2009b, "An Empirical Analysis of the Effect of Financial Distress on Trade Credit," IAE Business School *Working Paper*.

Myers, Stewart C., 1977, "Determinants of corporate borrowing," *Journal of Financial Economics* 5, 147–175.

Myers, S., and N. Majluf, 1984, "Corporate Financing and Investment Decisions When Firms Have Information that Investors Do Not Have," *Journal of Financial Economics* 13(2), 187–221.

Opler, T., L. Pinkowitz, R. Stulz, and R. Williamson, 1999, "The Determinants and Implications of Corporate Cash Holdings," *Journal of Financial Economics* 52, 3–46.

Pascale, R, 2009, Decisiones Financieras, Pearson Education, Buenos Aires, Argentina.

Petersen, M.A., and R.G. Rajan, 1997, "Trade Credit: Theories and Evidence," *Review of Financial Studies* 10, 661–691.

Porter, M., 1980, *Competitive Strategy*. The Free Press, New York, NY.

Preve, L., 2009, *Gestión de Riesgo: un enfoque estratégico*. Buenos Aires, Argentina: Editorial TEMAS.

Pulvino, T., 1998, "Do Asset Fire Sales Exist? An Empirical Investigation of the Commercial Aircraft Transactions," *Journal of Finance* 53, 939–978.

Ross, S. A., Westerfield, R.W., and Jordan, B. D., 2001, *Essentials of Corporate Finance*, Third Edition. McGraw—Hill, New York, N. Y.

Schmukler, S., and E. Vesperoni, 2000, "Globalization and Firms' Financing Choices: Evidence from Emerging Economies," *World Bank Policy Research Working Paper* 2323.

Schwartz, R.A., 1974, "An Economic Model of Trade Credit," *Journal of Financial and Quantitative Analysis*, September, 643–657.

Smith, J.K., 1987, "Trade Credit and Informational Asymmetry," *Journal of Finance* 42(4), 863–872.

Wilner, B., 2000, "The Exploitation of Relationships in Financial Distress: The Case of Trade Credit," *Journal of Finance* 55, 153–178.

# Index